The Sacred Wound

The Sacred Wound

Lois Gold, M.S.W.

FireWord Publishing, Inc.
www.firewordpublishing.com

A FireWord Book

Published by FireWord Publishing, Inc.
PO Box 4649
Portland, OR 97208
www.firewordpublishing.com

ISBN 1-930782-11-X

Cover art by Eric Busch
Street Art Productions

Book design by John Lauer

First published 2000

First printing 2000

Printed in the United States of America

DEDICATION

In Memory of

Elana Bess Gold

March 1, 1975 - September 29, 1991

Other Books by Author

Between Love & Hate: A Guide to Civilized Divorce

ACKNOWLEDGEMENTS

I wish to thank all those who kept me in their hearts and prayers when Elana died. To my friends Kristine Olson, Anita Lohman, Ruth Roth, and Bija Gutoff who entered the belly of this loss by reading early drafts of the manuscript, my special appreciation for their courage and commentary. Thank you to Ivan Gold, Elana's father, who lived it, and read it, and supported me and my writing, though our paths to healing were different. To Dorothy Wall, whose incisive and insightful editorial expertise stretched me as a writer, and weaned me from the expository therapist's voice to have the courage to tell my own story. To Natasha Kern, my agent, for her belief in this project, tireless effort, expert editorial advice, compassion, support, and friendship. And thank you to Laura Conner, at FireWord Publishing, whose outstanding production assistance and heart helped bring the book into its present form.

I wish to acknowledge the work of Jean Houston, whose brilliant treatises on mythology and psychology, introduced me to the concept of the sacred wound. It was through one of her seminars in which she discussed the theme of sacred wounding in mythology and the importance of connecting to the "larger stories" which govern our lives, that I found a way to move beyond my isolated identification with my loss.

And most importantly to Richard Forester, my partner in life, who lived through this with me, and without whom I would not have had the strength to heal.

Note: Readers who are interested in more information about the theme of *The Sacred Wound* are referred to Jean Houston's book, *The Search for the Beloved: Journeys in Mythology and Sacred Psychology.*

INTRODUCTION

This book is a memoir about the death of my only child at the age of sixteen. It is the story of the journey from unfathomable pain toward healing. Every parent's worst terror is that something might happen to their child. When the unthinkable happens, you believe you will die; and part of you does. Pain is your constant companion; it becomes your teacher. Compassion and love are the healers. And surrender is the dimly lit path through your grief.

I was just like everyone else until September 29, 1991, the day my daughter was killed in a plane crash in a small mountain community in Central Oregon. In one afternoon, the life I knew vaporized. I was plunged into an abyss. There was nothing in all my twenty years of professional experience as a therapist that prepared me or that I could call upon to help me survive.

Each act of surviving tragedy is an odyssey, terrifying and inspiring. We never expect to be called and nothing can prepare us for the journey into the underworld. This book is for those who are seeking meaning, solace, and a path to healing as I was. It is the story of everyone's journey back, and each one who returns lights the way for others.

The death of a child is a different order of suffering than anything else. The hand of fate has taken what is most cherished, that which is part of you, your biological core. It breaks your heart, it rips apart your soul. It shatters the fundamental ground on which you stand.

We accept the death of a parent because in the context of our cultural beliefs it is the natural order of life.

1

We mourn, revisit the past, deal with unfinished business, but ultimately accept it as natural, though never wanted. The death of a parent does not create a crisis of meaning. It may bring us closer to the issues of our own mortality and existential questions which we may not be ready to face, but it does not leave us shattered to the core. The death of a child violates the natural order. We have no cultural mechanisms or religious beliefs that help us to make sense out of a child dying, nor are there adequate customs or rituals to help the bereaved family. People gather around you for a while, but they go back to their own lives. Yours is never the same.

You have been singled out, whether you believe it is by chance or by a larger purpose and design. Primal trust is shattered, all that is familiar and known has been irretrievably altered. You are on your own. Your suffering and anguish open you to the questions of God, purpose, and the unanswerable why. You are forced to reconstruct life's meaning.

Loss that shatters one's life is a sacred wound, a wounding so profound, that it breaches the soul, penetrates the veils of who we are what we think life is about, and renders us available to the greater order. Like the mythological hero, who is wounded by forces from beyond, we, too, have been pierced by the fates, and our suffering opens us to questions we hadn't needed to ask before. As in all the great myths, it is out of the wounding that we grow into a larger sense of what life is about and are able to act accordingly.

You do not get over a sacred wound. You are transformed by it. Losing a child is a modern day initiation, and like some acolyte in an ancient initiation, you emerge from this ordeal another person, having given birth to a higher self that is unattainable to those who have not also undergone the ordeal.

I believe the path to wholeness is on the other side of anger, through an appreciation of the sacredness of your wound, that you have been pierced by the divine mystery

2

and thus opened to its grace. As Joseph Campbell says, the demon you swallow gives you its power. The greater life's pain, the greater life's reply.

As time goes on, you will begin to question how you are to live your life differently and how bearing the unbearable has recast you. Recovering from life-shattering loss is not about trying to regain the life you had. The question becomes why are you here. What is your purpose? How can you help others? People look at you differently; you are a reminder of life's fragility in their midst. Your priorities change at the deepest level. The path toward healing is the path of allowing your grief to open you to compassion and love, not to close you down in anger and despair.

The child who dies can be more the teacher in death than in life. A child's death discloses what you don't want to know. It shows you how understanding impermanence deepens the appreciation for what is around you, how being able to release that which you treasured most brings you closer to the higher principles and mysteries which govern our lives.

In the beginning, there is only pain. It is hard to believe there is anything beyond the immensity of your grief. For a long time there isn't. But tragedy carries a gift in its other hand and someday you will see this.

AUTHOR'S PREFACE

A book calls to you. You don't know where it will take you when you begin, just that you have to follow the call. This one took me by surprise. I had vehemently rejected the idea of writing about my daughter's death whenever it was suggested to me. I didn't keep a journal. Then one day almost two and a half years after her death, the realization that it was the right thing to do came to me in a flash. I didn't have to understand why, I just knew I had to do it. The title and form jumped out at me, and that afternoon I lit a candle, sat down at the computer and went back to that horrifying Sunday afternoon when it all began.

Writing anchored me and gave me purpose as well as catharsis and insight. I came to understand my experience as I wrote about it. I relived everything that glared back at me on that computer screen. As painful as it was, this was not a project that could be abandoned. I knew in completing this book, I would be symbolically completing something else, though it hadn't yet come into view.

As time went on, the writing became illuminating. I developed insights into the nature of healing as I reflected upon my travels and experiences in other cultures. I remember a well-known writer once commenting that she wrote to open into an experience and to learn, not to demonstrate what she knew.

The three mornings a week that were dedicated to writing gave me time to be with my loss and to regularly mark the page that says your life has fundamentally changed. I was not ready to go back to the life I had, and

I had no where else to go. Writing gave me a purpose at a time when the void in my life could have sapped all my strength. It gave me a way to give something to others. It was a very different experience than my previous book on non-adversarial divorce; that was a mission, the culmination of fifteen years of professional practice. I hovered over its success like a mother bird.

This book has been part of my own healing, and as such, I ask nothing for myself except that others may be helped by what I have been through. I am simply turning it over to the universe and trust that it will go where it needs to.

PART 1: IN THE BEGINNING

I sat on the patio that sunny Sunday morning drinking coffee and reading the *New York Times,* enjoying the last of the summer's warmth. My daughter, Elana, was at a cabin in the mountains in Eastern Oregon with her closest childhood friends. These four, Chessy, Liz, Kate and Elana, best friends through the sweetness, innocence, and hand holding of grade school, the capricious hurts, rejections, and yearnings of puberty, were now in their junior year of high school, reconciling who they were becoming with those childhood images. The weekend was like a rite of passage, a gathering for the first to turn seventeen, different, yet so much the same as all the birthdays they had shared since childhood.

I was allowing Elana to fly back early with Kate and her father in a private plane. It was a labored decision because I don't like small planes. But both girls were worried about being home to work on a major English paper which was on the computer and due on Monday. Kate's father, a pilot, welcomed the opportunity to fly out to pick them up. Chessy and Liz would drive home in the evening with Liz's parents. They were envious that Elana and Kate were going to fly.

Elana left for the weekend in a huff because I would not allow her to drive to the mountains herself and insisted she ride with Liz's parents. Torn between a commitment to her friend and the pressure of the English paper, she was angry that I could interfere with her already limited autonomy. As she was leaving, she kissed me goodbye, hugged me hastily and whispered, "I'm never coming home again." Her words hit me like a bullet, resonating with my worse fear, tapping my uneasiness about

9

allowing her to fly in a private plane. That her words could be a premonition was too terrifying a thought to endure. I convinced myself that I was responding to my own anxiety and her words were spoken as an angry adolescent prone to overstatement. I rationalized that it was a short trip on a sunny morning, the pilot, a family friend, was a cautious and conscientious person, and the co-pilot was an instructor. Flight time was only forty-five minutes. It would be all right I told myself. It wouldn't be fair to say no. I had to let her go. How many times can we clip our children's wings?

Elana was a child of divorce. I guess on some level I was always trying to make it up to her. She was three at the time, and by all standards, her father and I had a reasonably decent post-divorce relationship. But he soon remarried and moved to San Francisco, leaving me to be a single parent for most of her childhood. Each summer and Christmas vacation Elana spent time with her other family in San Francisco. By the time she was eight she was a seasoned traveler with her own frequent flyer card. It was not the way it was supposed to be, but that was the way it was. It was painful for her to have to say goodbye to one parent in order to be with the other. But we had gotten through all that. Her father and his family moved back to Portland a few years ago. She was part of two families now, navigating a life with three younger siblings in her father's home and being an only child with me. It was a contrast that had its share of challenges for us all, but Elana generally met them with surprising grace. And now we could breathe a sigh of relief, because despite the divorce, we had turned the corner on adolescence and had managed to turn out a bright, spirited, capable, charming young woman who was blossoming each day before our very eyes. But that was then. This was Sunday, September 29, 1991, the day that everything I understood about the world was shattered.

I looked at my watch as I sipped my morning coffee. I was uneasy. The plane was due in one more hour. Then

10

I could relax. Elana would be safe. I flipped through the travel section of the paper unable to concentrate. I tried to dismiss my anxiety by recalling all the times she had flown safely in commercial airlines and how I had learned to relax about that. Besides, she had promised to call me as soon as they landed at Hillsboro airport.

They were half an hour late. No call. I began to pace waiting for the phone to ring. I made myself wait another 15 minutes before I started to track them down. I didn't even know where to begin. I called Hillsboro airport, then Sisters airport. I was told to call the control tower. They had no information. My stomach was in a knot. Shuttled from airport to control tower to sheriff's office, I finally learned that there had been an accident at Sisters airport, involving an Osborne party. No details. I didn't know any Osborne. But this was too close for comfort. My heart was racing as I continued to try to get more information. All parties were evasive and unhelpful, until I screamed into the telephone that my sixteen year-old daughter was on a flight from Sisters to Hillsboro that was due an hour ago. Then they told me that a plane had crashed upon take-off involving a Moore and Osborne party and the only survivor was a teenager Elana Gold who was in critical condition at Bend General Hospital. Stu Moore, the pilot, his daughter Kate, and the co-pilot Keith Osborne had died. *Oh my God.*

I started calling. First Richard, the man whom I had been with for three years. He was just walking out the door to take his children on a hike. "Richard, we have to go to Bend. The plane crashed. Elana is in critical condition." Then I called Ivan, Elana's father, and two friends. I couldn't reach Judy Moore, the pilot's wife. I finally reached the neurologist at Bend General Hospital after being transferred four times. He explained Elana's condition and the emergency surgery they were about to perform to control the bleeding. I wondered why was I doing all the calling, why hadn't the authorities or the hospital called me? Finally Judy Moore called. She was at Hillsboro

11

airport waiting to pick up Stu and the girls and wondered if I had heard anything about the plane being late. There was a veiled anxiety in her voice. How do you tell your friend that her worst fears have been confirmed, that her husband and daughter have just died? "Judy, I don't know what happened. It crashed upon take-off in a farmer's field just beyond the runway. Elana is the only one who is alive... Let me call someone to come get you...let me do something...I'm so sorry...."

My insides liquified. Three people were dead, my daughter, my only child, was in critical condition in a hospital four hours away. All I knew was that I had to save her. I had to get the best medical help I could. I called my friend who was the head of the emergency department at a large Portland hospital. "Lindsey," I cried frantically, "the plane crashed, Elana's in a coma, they are about to perform emergency neurosurgery. I don't understand the procedures they are doing. Please can you call the neurosurgeon for me? What if they aren't doing the right thing? Bend is not a big city. This isn't a major hospital. I'll die if anything happens to her. Lindsey you have to help save her."

For the next hour I was on the telephone with Lindsey, Elana's neurosurgeon in Bend, her father. She was in a coma, serious edema, swelling on the brain, a broken femur and wrist, spine OK. Traumatic head injury, collapsed lung; the next 24 hours were critical. If she makes it through the night, she has a chance. I was in adrenalin overdrive, numb but functioning, until the neurologist called back as they were prepping her for surgery. He asked if Elana had a large scar on her abdomen. The air rushed out of my lungs...Elana had no scars. Kate had an abdominal scar from a surgery when she was a child. Oh my god, Kate was the one on the operating table. *Elana was dead.*

I couldn't speak, I couldn't move. I was still holding the receiver in my hand when Elana's father arrived. We fell into each other's arms and wailed. I don't know how long we stood there desperately clutching each other. Suddenly I got up. I had to call Judy to tell her that her daughter was alive. The line was busy. I jumped into the car and drove the mile to her house. The second she opened the door, I blurted it out—"the girls' identities have been confused. Kate is in the hospital. Elana is...." We grabbed each other and sobbed as if the knife went through both our hearts. As I pulled away, we looked into each other's anguished eyes trying to absorb this sudden reversal of fate. Finally, Judy said to me, "We have one daughter between us now."

It is as if the bowels of the earth open and suck you in. You enter another dimension. Time stops. You are a fractal of your former self. You are split into a thousand pieces. Nothing is real.

I think that if I had been told outright that Elana was dead and hadn't had those two hours of preparation dealing with the neurosurgeon, I would have collapsed at the news or been in a rage, a wild woman smashing everything in sight. As it was, I was in shock, but my body held together. It's odd how things happen. I don't remember much about the next twenty-four hours. Everyone came, everyone took over.

Is She Calling, Is She Crying?

That night I fell into a strange sleep. The horrific reality of the day vanished like a dream and the reverie of sleep became the most wanted reality. I awoke with a start in the middle of the night to a bird screeching outside the bedroom window. *SQUAWK, SQUAWK, SQUAWK, SQUAWK.* It was an unearthly sound, shrill, terror struck, beckoning. I had never in my life heard a bird make a sound like that, and certainly never in the middle of the night. It was the sound of death. I knew. Elana was crying out in pain. My pain, her pain...I knew.

I got out of bed and walked from window to window.

13

I couldn't see anything. I went out on the back deck. The sky was black and clear and not a sound could be heard. Shivering, arms wrapped around myself to keep warm, heart pounding, I waited. The night quaked with my expectancy, but nothing more happened. Finally, I went inside, climbed back into bed and into Richard's arms, "That *was* her, you know."

The next night, China, one of the kittens from our litter of Himalayans, the one Elana had named and I had decided to keep after the accident, woke me at 3:00 a.m. mewing plaintively and insistently licking my face. Her raw tongue migrated across my cheek with a determination and purpose beyond her own needs. She mewed and licked, mewed and licked, and mewed and licked. If she could have cried human tears, she would have, if she could have said the words, "I love you," she would have. I welcomed her into my arms, burying my tears in her softness. I knew this was from Elana. I had never seen a cat cry or behave like this in a lifetime of being around them. This 3:00 a.m. lament went on for six months like clockwork. I was so bold as to tell my friends this kitten either picked up Elana's presence or Elana was communicating through this kitten. I am sure people thought I was crazy, but some things you just know.

The Rabbi

I called out for the Rabbi. I wasn't religious, I didn't believe in God, and yet he was the one I wanted by my side. My world had shattered, my heart was split open, and I stood frozen in time and space. I didn't know where the ground was. I didn't know how to move my feet. The Rabbi was going to be my lifeline. He would know how to maneuver in this black hole. He could explain death, he could tell me why, he would tell me what to do, he would have the answers, he would give me a reason to keep living, he could yell at God for me, he could petition on my behalf, he could...do something. I was powerless.

The Rabbi came. His face was pained and troubled. There was a sorrow in his eyes that was ancient. I needed to be near him. The idea of my daughter being dead was incomprehensible, unspeakable, unacceptable. I desperately grasped for any metaphysical knowledge or evidence that would diminish the finality that death had always represented to me. "Talk to me, give me something to hang on to," I cried. The Rabbi told me that in Judaism, the soul is eternal. I couldn't begin to comprehend what he meant, but it was what I wanted to hear. He told me it was important to distinguish between mourning for Elana and mourning for me. That made sense because, at that point, my darkest tears were for the enormity of her loss— a life so full of promise cut short, a life so short of experiences that now would never be.

When I fell to my knees in self-recrimination for allowing her to travel in a private plane against my better judgement, he gently held my hand and helped me to stop turning my despair against myself. All I could say was WHY. Why did this happen? What have I done? What did she mean when she said "I'm never coming home again?" DID SHE KNOW? DO WE KNOW ? He tried to help me see that there are no answers to why things like this happen. There is no ultimate answer to the question, WHY? It is a question born of despair, grief, and helplessness, and while I might need to keep asking and searching, it is an endless loop. Eventually, I would have to accept the fact that there is no answer. While this didn't quiet the burning in my mind, I acknowledged that I might never find the answers I sought.

When I sat lifeless on the couch staring vacantly at the lawn where just a few days earlier Elana was kicking a soccer ball, he took my hand and gently told me that our children are gifts. They are lent to us, we do not own them. We are given no guarantees. Nothing is permanent. Zen is fine in the abstract, I thought, but it is another matter to confront the issue of impermanence so brutally in relation to your deepest attachment. I simply wasn't ready to hear this, but I knew it was true and I appreciated being reminded of one of life's most difficult realities. Lastly, he told me not to hold in my grief, not to have to be strong to protect other people. He gave me permission to be real.

I am profoundly grateful to Rabbi Emannual Rose. More than anyone that first week, it was his wisdom and compassionate presence that held me together and gave me ground on which to stand. It is something I will never forget.

Seeing Her for the Last Time

There would be no open casket. But we could see her at the funeral home. I was told that there were head lacerations and that her face had been disfigured. Could I stand looking at the mortician's reconstruction of the sweetness and innocence of her smile? Could I stand to see the dark eyes once dancing and full of mischief closed forever? Could I stand the stillness? Could I stand death? I was afraid of the encounter, but I knew I wanted to be with her no matter what. I knew I wanted to hold her no matter what. I had to talk to her no matter what. She was part of me. All I wanted was to be near her again.

We drove to the funeral parlor together, Richard, Ivan, Elana's step-mother, Trudi, and I. We each spent time alone with her. I went to enter the viewing room first. I stood in the doorway unable to move. There she was across the room, my only child, lying upon a raised platform of white satin pillows, draped in a simple linen shroud according to tradition. Her hands were folded on her chest. I was entering another dimension. All pulsation in my body ceased. Air did not pass through my lungs. The penetrating stillness of death made this room feel holy.

I could barely walk toward her. The last time I had

seen her, she was wearing cowboy boots, tattered jeans, long beaded earrings and had a colorful Guatemalan purse slung over her shoulder. She had exuded life. How could the barrier between life and death be so fragile? How could she be laughing and exuberant one moment and so deeply silenced the next? This couldn't be real.

Oddly, I felt comforted to be with her. I studied the injuries on her face, the reconstruction of her nose and lips, the bruises on her hands. I soothed her brow. I held her hands for a long time, embedding their ethereal gracefulness in my mind forever. The hands I had held and soothed so many times before. Now they were cold. I thought about how these lovely long fingers first reached across the keys of the piano, then danced on the scales of the flute. I had always been struck by the beauty of Elana's hands and I didn't want to ever forget what they looked like. I moved down to her feet and rubbed them as if the power of my touch could restore life into the soft, cold flesh. I put my head on her chest as she had done so many times on mine. I wanted to cradle her in my arms and carry her back to her room, just as I did when she was a little girl and had fallen asleep in my bed. Oh Elana, come home, please come home. I need you with me. I need to talk and laugh about the things we used to. We didn't have a chance to say goodbye. How could you be gone? This is a bad dream. I know I'll wake up and drive you to school tomorrow.

I didn't want to leave the mortuary, but there was nothing else to do. I couldn't take her with me. I sat and stroked her and cried and told her how much I loved her until there was no strength left in me.

Forever Sixteen

The darkest hour was the day before the funeral. Richard's mother called me from Toronto. Her voice was soothing and knowing. I will never forget the impact of her words when she said to me, "Elana will be forever sixteen. She'll always have the unblemished beauty and innocence of youth—she'll be spared life's hardships. Some of us can watch our children grow up, but your daughter will remain as she always was." Her words were like catching a bullet in your teeth. A sob came out of me from deep in the belly, from that place where truth penetrates the very soul.

Forever sixteen. These words were imprinted in my psyche, never to be forgotten, a stitch in the rip in my heart, giving me something where I had nothing. Yes, from now on Elana would be forever sixteen. Perhaps if anyone else had said this, it would have been an empty platitude; but coming from Irene, spoken with the authority of experience, these words commanded attention. They resonated with the wisdom and compassion of one who has been there. And she had. She had survived the Holocaust. What would have been her high school years were spent in the Warsaw Ghetto hiding in abject terror and near starvation. She finally escaped with false papers to a French labor camp. Yes, Irene knows about loss and survival. She gave up Richard, her only child, to the safety of her parents and wasn't able to reclaim him until he was twelve. She went on to get two law degrees, made her way to America, and became a law professor.

Forever sixteen, the most poignant and absolute truth about Elana, was sad but soothing. It was the poetic notion that defined her anew, gave me the starting place to open my heart, and gave us all a way for her to live on.

Anguished Choices

Later that day, the funeral director called and asked if there was anything of Elana's that I wanted to put in the casket with her. Like a madwoman, I rummaged through her room, throwing open drawers and closet doors. "We should be packing for college," I screamed. "She should

18

be taking all her favorite things. No mother should be choosing what to lay in a coffin next to her child." I stood in the center of her room in a fury looking at her ribbons and bows, earrings, stuffed animals, her posters, weavings, and drawings on the wall. The anesthetic of shock was wearing off. The physical act of taking things that were quintessential Elana and putting them in a brown paper bag for the funeral director was like having my flesh ripped apart with bare hands. I couldn't do it. I threw myself across her bed, tearing at the sheets, my body racked with sobs. I think it was the worst pain I will ever know. I didn't want to live. My sister- in-law, Barbara, tried to calm me. She brought me some tea, held my hand and said I didn't have to do this. But, I wanted Elana to have things that she cared about with her. Finally, I was able to stand up again and chose her running shoes, her favorite hat, a stuffed animal, Grateful Dead tapes, and an unmatched pair of earrings, one blue and silver and the other strands of tiny white beads with pieces of fresh water pearls. I very deliberately put their mates on her teddy bear which still sits on her bed wearing her other favorite hat. Beyond the symbolism of having one of each pair of earrings going with her and one remaining here, in my heart I hoped beyond hope that her incorporeal spirit might come back and turn the earrings on the teddy bear into a matched set.

The Funeral

It was the morning of the funeral. I didn't know how I was going to get through it. I had always hated funerals. Death scared me, but this was different. The worst possible thing had already happened. There was nothing else to fear.

The family drove to the synagogue together and gathered in a small ante room. We were led into the sanctuary through a special entrance. The sight was overwhelming. Sunlight filtered through the stained glass windows on a profusion of color. The sanctuary was ablaze with flowers. Elegant arrangements of purple delphiniums, yellow mums, delicate salmon colored lilies, white roses, crimson cosmos, scarlet orchids, giant star gazer lilies, golden sunflowers bursting with fall's first touch. These grand bouquets filled the entire front area of the dais and the steps leading down to the sanctuary. I just stared at the flowers, overcome by this extraordinary outpouring, all for Elana, my sweet, sweet Elana. Oh Elana, I thought, look how people care about you. Look at these flowers! My heart wept to see her honored with such beauty and bounty. It made me realize that she had a special way of connecting with people. She was free-spirited, warm and open hearted, with an unselfconscious honesty and wit that were endearing. A teacher once said she was like a ray of sunlight in the room. Elana touched people even in brief encounters. Now, I could see this was her gift. She was a loving soul and it was coming back to her.

Then, my eyes moved up to the bimah. There in stark contrast stood the casket, solitary, elevated, covered with a royal blue velvet sheath with the emblem of the Star of David on it. The image was powerful, painful, and in its own way quite beautiful. It beheld the holy separation between us now. Just three years before, Elana had stood on this same bimah reciting from the Torah for her Bat Mitzvah. Tall, lovely, stepping forward into life. I closed my eyes. The reality of my child in a casket was excruciating.

I turned my head and looked around. The synagogue was filled to capacity, even the balcony. I was told there were more than 1,000 people. I saw my close friends. I saw the grief-stricken faces of people I used to know, of colleagues I hadn't seen in years, of her classmates, her best friends, their parents, people who had known her since she was an infant. This community was in deep mourning, in shock over the death of an innocent, open-hearted, life-affirming bright one. It could happen to them.

I declined to ride in the front seat of the hearse on the way to the cemetery. Instead, I climbed in the back and laid my head on the coffin. I wanted to be near Elana for as long as I could under any circumstances. If I thought I could have gotten away with it, I would have brought her body home. I couldn't bear to be separated so suddenly and harshly, the umbilical cord that is never wholly severed to be so brutally wrenched. I fantasized commandeering the hearse and forcing the chauffeur to exit the interstate. We would leave the funeral procession far behind and drive into the clouds.

As I sat crouched in the back of the hearse with my head resting on the coffin, I thought about how Elana would want this occasion to be. It had to be less serious and solemn. It had to have her imprimatur on it. So I took out the deep red lipstick she had given me for Mother's Day. I put some on and handed it to Trudi, her step-mother. We planted kisses all over this plain pine box. Her coffin began to look like the cover of an old Rolling Stone album. I knew she would like this. Elana liked to amuse and be amused. Like most adolescents, she cultivated her own style of responding to the world. She teased the boundaries of what was expected with just the right amount of irony. She left this realm soaring into the sunlight waving at her friends from an airplane which turned toward the heavens, never to return.

The White Butterfly

We assembled at the Beth Israel cemetery, a few miles from town. It was one of those perfect September days, warm, clear, not a cloud in the sky. The sun shone gloriously and with equanimity on this circle of grief. Yellow school buses could be seen in the distance behind the trees. I looked around. Everything was one teary blur. I remember thinking school buses don't belong in cemeteries.

The rabbi continued the service. The cantor sang the prayers as we stood solemnly at the grave side. The plain pine coffin, now sealed with ruby red kisses was mechanically suspended slightly above the ground. I stared at it, motionless. She couldn't be in there. The sight was unendurable.

At the close of the service according to Jewish tradition each family member shovels a mound of earth over the casket before it is lowered into the ground. Elana's father went first, sighing deeply, a stifled sob escaping. As he handed me the shovel, something inside snapped. No requirement of ceremony could contain my emotion as I held that shovel in my hand. Every atom in my body protested, *I was not going to put my daughter underground.* Gripped by the singular force of emotional truth, I cried out loud, "Elana is not in that casket. Her spirit is free, she soars like the wind, she will always be with us. ELANA IS NOT IN THAT GRAVE." I refused for this pine box to contain all there was of her. But perhaps in that moment of raging agony, of circuits on fire, I glimpsed the truth of the soul's journey. And a little white butterfly circled the group, lighting from time to time, as if visiting and nodding approval.

When I looked up, I saw her friends and classmates, their faces drawn and pale, huddled together holding each other's hands. I invited them to write and draw on the casket. This was not the tradition. But something inside me knew that tradition was inadequate to express the grief in this gathering of so many young people. One by one, then in pairs and groups of three, they crouched on the ground, their heads bent over their hands as they wrote their goodbyes. The casket became Elana's yearbook, strewn with roses, poetry and words of love. When the last child stood up and silently filed back to the circle, I desperately wanted to brush aside the flowers and read what they had written. I yearned to know that Elana's time here mattered and that she would be missed. But this was for them, it was their remembrance and their goodbye. Yearbooks are supposed to be enjoyed in the future, but this one would be closed now and forever. How I wished that Elana could see what had been written. And the little white butterfly lingered.

This was the first appearance of the white butterfly. It has come many times since. I could say it was and has been a symbol of Elana's spirit. But in my heart, I know the mysteries of the soul are little understood, and the butterfly as just a "symbol" is far too narrow an explanation.

Prayers

Friends and family came to the house after the funeral. I walked in the door to see a spectacular array of food that would have befitted a celebration. Through my tears, all I could say was how Elana would want to be here. Looking at the pasta salads, Greek olives, sun dried tomatoes, polenta and black beans, dark rich breads, platters of cut-up fruit, pastries and strudels, I knew she would have been excited by this veritable feast, uttering her trademark, "yum." It brought a smile to my face. It was the first time in four days I had smiled.

Meanwhile Kate lay unconscious in a coma at St. Charles General Hospital in Bend, 200 miles away. She had undergone five simultaneous emergency surgical procedures the Sunday she was admitted, and she remained in critical condition. The prognosis was very guarded. I talked to Judy every day to see how Kate was doing. We were all on edge about when and even whether she would regain consciousness.

As the sun began to set, I asked everyone to come out to the back yard to form a prayer circle for Kate. I had seen this done for a colleague who was losing her sight. It gave her the strength to successfully pull through a difficult surgery. There was a hesitation as this quite conventional group of friends filed out the door. I called Judy to tell her that we were about to send energy and prayers for Kate. We held hands and closed our eyes, as I guided this gathering in a meditation to reach into the silence of their faith to send prayers and healing to Kate and her family. Later people asked me how could I do this when my own loss was so all consuming. I thought, how could I not?

Sitting Shiva

Sitting Shiva is Judaism's mourning ritual. For seven days the bereaved remain at home to honor the dead and allow family and friends to pay their respects. Mourner's Kaddish, a daily prayer requiring the presence of ten people, referred to as a minion, is said each morning and evening that week. People gathered at my house with the rabbi and the cantor, but I have few recollections of these comings and goings before the funeral except for the prayer circles for Kate.

After the funeral, the family went to Ivan's house each morning to recite the Kaddish. The service was led by a young, orthodox rabbi whom I had never met. He was draped in the traditional prayer shawl, with Phylacteries, the tiny black leather boxes which hold miniature prayer scrolls, hanging over his eyes and bound around his arms. Even though I am not religious, these were familiar prayers, said for both of my parents, Ivan's father, and various aunts and uncles over the years. Always for old people. I had never recited them for a child.

The dining room table had coffee and pastries set out on Ivan's finest china. Pictures of Elana and his three other children, Jonathan, Lauren, and Matthew hung over the fireplace. This gathering brought back childhood memories of visiting distant relatives who were sitting Shiva when I'd go to see my grandparents with my family. Often I didn't even know who had died, but I would be dutifully taken along because I was the young one, the spark of life. I remember the somber feeling in those dark

24

Philadelphia row houses. Mirrors covered, drapes drawn, a memorial candle burning, old women with anguished eyes and fleshy arms, old men fixed to their chairs sitting silently in the shadows. A dark mahogany table covered with a lace tablecloth, dishes of herring, rughala, coffee cake, rye bread, chopped liver, dill pickles. Eat, eat, they'd say. Have some rye bread, as if taking in food could fill the emptiness.

Here at Ivan's, perched high upon a hillside, the vista of the city opening before us, the snow- capped mountains in full view and bright sunlight streaming in the picture windows, one would not immediately recognize this as a house of mourning. But there was the dark mahogany table, white linen, fine china, coffee cake, herring, chopped liver, rye bread, dill pickles. Now I was on the other side of that mahogany table. Eat, eat, I said. My turn to be the house of mourning had come.

Ivan's family was there. His mother and his aunt, his brother and his former sister-in-law and cousins who had flown in from the east coast. Both my parents are dead and I am an only child, but I had remained close to Ivan's family even after the divorce. Trudi, Elana's step-mother, and her family were also there. Ivan and Trudi were separated. They had been married for thirteen years, and Ivan and I had been married the ten years before that. It was a strange gathering of ex-relatives. Sometimes death binds stronger than life. There was no feeling of being an "ex" anything.

The rabbi led the prayers, we had coffee and pastries and talked about Elana. My mother-in-law, Leah, and her sister, Esther, both in their eighties, paced nervously, wringing their hands. This was not the first time Ivan's family was mourning the loss of a young bright one. Esther's grandson, Jacob, was killed on a motor scooter in England when he was twenty-one just after graduating from college there. Now each had lost a grandchild. I looked at these women, who were robust, energetic, and still sharp as a whistle. Their eyes were beginning to reveal the toll life had taken. I could see that Elana's death had brought back the memory of their sister, Charlotte, who died when she was seventeen. She had been the baby of the family, and was said to been the prettiest and most talented of the three. It was apparent their tears could be stirred even sixty-five years later. I thought about all the times my mother-in-law had spoken with such sadness of her sister and yet, to me, she had remained the anonymous "one who died." Now I knew better.

Classical music usually filled Ivan's house. One morning after coffee, he played a recording of Rod Stewart's *Forever Young* with the volume turned all the way up.

I sat back in an overstuffed chair, gripping the arms and thinking, oh my God, this is Elana. This is all there is...forever young. There is no more. Ivan paced the floor crying, pounding his fist into the palm of his hand. *FOREVER YOUNG...FOREVER YOUNG...FOREVER YOUNG...* Sound flashed like a neon sign in my face—your daughter will grow into life no further, she will never see a day unfold again... *FOREVER YOUNG...FOREVER YOUNG...FOREVER YOUNG...*melodic, penetrating, insistent, stinging my soul. There was no solace in this poetry. Finally, I couldn't hold it back. The moan came from deep in my belly, the protest that had been burning inside since the moment the neurosurgeon uttered the words, "I'm so sorry, your daughter has died." I fell to my knees wailing, "NO, NO, NO, NOOOOOOOO...NOT ELANA...NOT ELANA...."

There are no words for the agony I felt as I lay curled on the floor while the chorus, *FOREVER YOUNG, FOREVER YOUNG...*blasted from every corner of the room. Then I became quiet. I looked at the vista through the enormous bay window and thought, I could back up against the living room wall and in two giant steps leap through. I saw myself in slow motion crashing through the plate glass, suddenly thrust into another dimension. Floating in space, beyond this pain, towards Elana. I could do it, I thought. The other side of life held an appeal for me now, not terror. Snapping back to reality, my head still spinning, I moved away from the window. I was coming close to the edge.

Refusing Death

Her death stirred a protest inside me that came from the belly of the earth. All my instincts rose up against her absence. I held on as tight as I could, adorning myself with her presence. I wore her clothes, her jewelry, her perfume and the gifts she had given me. I kept a photo of her against my heart under my clothes. I never took off a wooden bracelet she had made for me on the lathe in the fifth grade. I began to wear her signature ring and the silver bracelet given to her by her father for her Bat Mitzvah. I refused to go anywhere without feeling as if I were taking her with me. She was still my daughter. I wasn't going to leave her behind.

I left her favorite food in the pantry, the mini-onion bagels and raisin bread in the freezer. Her soccer shoes remained where she left them outside the back door, her running shoes on the front seat of my car. I wanted her things to stay exactly where they were, the book bag on the floor in her room, her toiletries, makeup and knick-knacks by her sink, even the dirty socks on her closet floor. I didn't feel I had to explain or justify it to anyone. Later, whenever I traveled, I took a packet of photographs of her to share with colleagues. These rituals of always wearing an article of her clothing, a gift she had given me, and traveling with her photos continued for over two years. I can't even remember for how many months I left her running shoes on the seat of my car.

There are little shrines we erect, little pieces of them we will keep forever, things that we try to hold inside. These are things that say our child is not gone. They are the ties we are not ready to break. Maybe some day we will, or maybe we won't. I think either way it is all right.

27

Elana's closest friends were at the house almost every day that first week with their families. They were in shock. Chessy and Liz had just spent a wonderful weekend in the mountains with Kate and Elana, riding horses, goofing around, celebrating Liz's seventeenth birthday. Then they were there at the airport watching the plane take off, waving goodbye from the runway to Kate and Elana in their silly girlish way, envious that they couldn't go with them, when a few seconds later, the motor cut off. They saw the Life Flight helicopter. They went to the hospital. They knew before I did.

That first week was all a blur to me. Lots of other classmates and friends came and went. I told them all they could go into Elana's room and take something, a piece of clothing, jewelry, art work, whatever. But Chessy Stevenson, Liz Sowles and Erika Kinney, these three, were the special ones. They loved Elana dearly. We'd go into her room together, look through her closet, hold each other and cry. It was all so unreal. Like me, they couldn't let her go. Her clothes were the closest link to Elana in the flesh. Each article of clothing carried a story for them. *She was wearing this when we went to the Santana concert....I was with her when she bought this sweater and we argued over who saw it first and could get it....Oh no, here's the blue linen dress she wore for eighth grade graduation....* Clothes, the lifeblood of female adolescence were now the closest link to the friend they loved. Chessy took some T-shirts because they still carried Elana's scent. Later, she told me she never washed them. They all wanted her trademark cowboy boots which they agreed to share, each taking a turn every few weeks. But what they really wanted was a piece of Elana, something to hold on to, something that said, "she is not gone."

In the middle of all these coming and goings, the phone rang. "Hi, is Elana there?" said a tentative male voice. "Who is this please?" I asked, steeled for what had to come next. It was her friend Mike, a young man she had met during the summer at ski racing camp on the snow fields of Mt. Hood. He lived in New York state and called frequently. She'd settle into her room with the door closed, always emerging with a smile. *Hi, is Elana there?* Never in a million years does a seventeen year old expect to hear what I had to say. "Mike, I don't know how to tell you...there was a plane crash...she died immediately." He couldn't speak. I told him how much I knew Elana enjoyed talking with him and that I would send him some pictures and a memento. All he could utter was how sorry he was. The next day a beautiful bouquet of flowers arrived. For days I thought about this poor kid, the shocked silence at the other end of the phone 3,000 miles away, isolated from the support of other grief-stricken friends. I hoped he was all right. I wished I could have met him. I thought about all the boys I would never get to meet, all the boys she would never get to meet.

The Last Photo Op

The dining room table served up her life. A collage of photos was strewn from one end to the other. It was the stopping place to visit Elana. From the day of the funeral it remained this way for a month. Amidst a bouquet of pink roses rested the story of a life: the baby who could smile on command sitting in a miniature bentwood rocker; at three months propped on the couch with the *New Yorker* magazine in her hands; in her high chair at one year spattered with the first taste of birthday cake; in pink tutu and ballet shoes smelling a flower; cartwheels in the backyard with four other little cherubs; on the patio with her grandparents balancing the new kitten on her head; slumber parties eight abreast on the living room floor; running under the sprinklers with our big white sheepdog; waving goodbye from the yellow school bus as she left for summer camp; at her Bat Mitzvah party in the wide brimmed straw hat and flowered dress as pubescence gave way to feminine allure; in my navy blue suit jacket and jeans at the freshman sports awards dinner, her hair pinned back in a bun the way my father always loved mine; in our driveway with Chessy and Liz, car keys in hand, posing next to a red octagonal stop sign they swore they found lying on the side of the road; outside a Parisian boulangerie with a loaf of French bread sticking out of her purse; in Monet's garden, at the Louvre—all the photos from her trip to France this past summer with Liz, the trip she wanted to use her money for now and not wait until she was older.

Dominating this collage, resting against the wall, almost as big as life, was a 16x20 enlargement of her skiing down the mountain on a bright sunny day in a slalom competition. Wind swept hair, Ray Ban sunglasses, zinc-coated lips, leaning into the mountain as she angled around the gate to shave seconds off her time, turquoise jacket open at the neck and billowing in the wind—she looked strong, beautiful, invincible. That was how I wanted to remember her.

And finally there were the rolls of film that were retrieved from the crash site. This was the last time the girls were together. Posing on horses, sitting sweetly arms and legs entwined on benches in the woods, dallying amidst the lodge pole pines with the snow capped volcanic peaks of the Cascades in the distance. They were strong, vigorous with the fresh outdoorsy look of growing up in Oregon, and deeply connected to each other. Little did they know this was the last photo op. Finding Kate and Elana's cameras amongst the wreckage and having reprints made was an obsession for Liz and Chessy. This was the last vestige of how it was. There would be no more pictures of Elana.

Acute grief. The clinical words are shock, disorienta-
tion, numbness, a sense of unreality. I felt as if I were in a
time warp. I couldn't feel myself. There was an unreality
to everything. A force other than my own intention carried me through each day. I could see the physicality of
my body, but if you looked into my eyes, you would see no
one was there. I was sleepwalking, able to function only
because others were around. A house full of friends and
family kept me from becoming completely invisible to
myself. I wondered what I was going to do when they went
home. I was incapable of returning to work. All I could see
were the four walls closing in on me. Staying in the house
without Elana at this point in time would have put me
over the edge.

So Richard and I went to Portugal. It was a trip that
had been scheduled for a year. I was going to cancel, but
friends advised me to wait the week out. Now it became a
necessary distraction instead of the long anticipated vacation. As we walked through the airport and boarded the
plane, I felt I was moving in cyberspace. Recognizable
images were everywhere, but I was outside their realm. I
clutched a long- stemmed red rose which a friend had given
me to remind me of Elana's love. My carry-on luggage
was an unnecessary appendage to which I paid little attention, dropping and dragging it through three airports;
but for twelve hours I *never* let go of the rose.

The first part of the trip was a retreat for therapists
who had worked with Virginia Satir, a pioneer in the field
of family therapy. The group continued to meet even after
her death. I would be seeing many old friends from all
over the country. I will never forget walking into the room,
amidst the joyous greetings, hugs, and how are yous. I
took off my sunglasses and said, "Elana was killed in a
plane crash two weeks ago. I decided to come anyway because I couldn't stand being at home alone." In that in-

stant their faces turned horror struck. They put their arms around me in comfort and love, and a bond was formed that has lasted to this day.

I didn't teach or attend any of the seminars. I slept, visited with friends, walked on the beach with Richard, and wept. I was in a world of my own, passing time. I didn't know what to do with myself. Strange coincidences occurred which made me feel that Elana was around me. The first night, I was awakened before dawn by an eerie play of lights on the wall. I lay in bed mesmerized by the shadowy movements. There was a strange stillness and thickness in the air. Time seemed to stop. I felt a presence. I didn't dare move. Was this my imagination or was her spirit here? After a while I climbed out of bed and looked out the window to see if I could find the source of this strange light, but I couldn't see anything.

The next day I went for a run on the beach by myself. I ran barefoot along the water's edge, staring out at the vastness of the Atlantic. As my silent tears gave way to breathless, heaving sobs, a flock of birds suddenly appeared from beyond the horizon. They accompanied me along the shore line for at least a mile before turning away. I felt that Elana was saying "Here I am. See, I am not alone. I am free." Birds continued to mysteriously flock to me whenever I was alone on the beach thinking of her. I took comfort in these strange coincidences. I knew they had to do with Elana.

The wine at dinner seemed to take the edge off my detachment and I would have a momentary lapse into a familiar sense of self. Once I even got up to dance, though a small voice said, how could you be dancing two weeks after your daughter died? But this was no ordinary dancing. Elana's love of music thrust me onto that dance floor. I was dancing for Elana because she couldn't. The injustice of a mother carrying on in place of her daughter raged through the soles of my feet. At one point, turning from Richard on the crowded dance floor, I locked eyes with a young pretty girl about twenty. We began shaking and shimmying, smiling radiantly, following each other's lead. As the drum riff went on, the energy between us became electric. We never took our eyes off each other. After a while it wasn't really me dancing. Elana was dancing me. I was in ecstacy, communing with my child's spirit, dancing my heart out with a young girl who reminded me of her. When it was over, we hugged. There were no words for what we had experienced. It came from somewhere else.

After the retreat, Richard and I rented a car and traveled up north. We drove through spectacular scenery, hilltop cathedrals, quaint old fishing villages, and walled cities with narrow cobblestone streets. I tried to take in the castles, medieval fortress, and colorful old men sitting outside cafes puffing on their pipes. It was all a two-dimensional image on a blank screen. When I was away from the group, alone with Richard, with no one to help distract us and keep us afloat, it was difficult to infuse each other with energy. I wondered how this would ultimately affect our relationship. Richard was subdued, but also protective and solicitous. It was as though I had just come out of intensive care. I'm sure he was worried about whether I would recover. We had moments of extraordinary closeness, but mostly I was numb.

The only thing that made me come alive were the artisan shops where I would look for presents to bring back to the people who were so kind and loving towards me. I noticed that when my heart was engaged in extending love, I was not in pain. This need to give momentarily shoved grief aside. At the time, I didn't understand the significance of this discovery, but the simple act of choosing gifts gave me peace and joy. It differed from a giving that comes from propriety, obligation, or the need to be well-thought of, as in "we need to pick up a bottle of wine to take to dinner." These gifts were intrinsically linked to the message of love, and, as I later discovered, these loving acts, the opening of your heart to others, is the first crossroad in grief's dark journey. It is easy to miss it.

I returned home from Portugal, not with the usual feeling of being recharged that comes from a wonderful vacation, but more able to face the house and the loneliness without the emptiness sapping all my strength.

Flowers

The funeral bouquets lingered as the shock set in. Even after I had been gone two weeks, the house remained a garden of fragrance and color. Magnificent floral arrangements sat on every table and counter top. Their sheer beauty inspired a sense of the divine. I had a physiological need to be near these flowers. I bathed my face in the sweet fragrances. I brushed the velvety blooms across my cheeks. With my heart so dark, they were my only connection to the Light.

Sitting at the dining room table, I would find myself drawn into the mystery of existence while absently contemplating the beauty of a bouquet. Always, there would be a shift in consciousness, a shift of perception, and I would see the essence of Elana's spirit in the flowers. It was as if she became a flower. When the funeral bouquets faded, the house became as dark and empty as my broken heart. The new bouquets that graced the table each week were my private memorial to Elana. If I looked at them just right, I could always see her.

As the weeks wore on, I found myself strangely magnetized to flowers. I studied the faded blooms of neighboring gardens thinking how I would have a garden like that next year. I found myself staring at the rows of rose bushes planted alongside the sidewalk on city streets. I was even taken in by the fall colors of the landscaping along the highway. A flower was no longer simply a flower to me, but a reflection of the omnipresent bounty and mystery of existence, a window into the sacred that Elana opened and I walked through. Her death was giving me deeper eyes.

Then one day while rummaging through Elana's book bag, I found sketches of flowers on a piece of paper with the caption, "I live for flowers."

Kate

Kate Moore and Elana had been friends since preschool. When they were younger, it was usually Kate who came to the beach with us for the weekend, or it was Kate and Elana dressing up for Halloween, or Kate and Elana working on a school project. Then there was Kate and Elana on the soccer, track and cross country teams, and finally Kate and Elana driving each other to school. Now Kate was in a coma and Elana was dead.

I was haunted by the vision of them in the back seat of the plane the instant their excitement turned to horror, clutching each other's hands, screaming, *Oh, my God.* I knew that these girls, who had held each other's hands a thousand times before, were holding hands in the last shattering moment.

As soon as I returned from Portugal, I called Judy in Bend to see if Kate had emerged from the coma. I had a strange feeling she would open her eyes the day I was leaving for Portugal and had sent her roses with a note the morning of my departure. Judy sounded cheerful and reported that Kate was out of intensive care. She thanked me for the roses. Then, in a tentative voice, she said that Kate had regained consciousness the day of my departure as I had foretold in the note. She was a little spooked by this uncanny coincidence. So was I, but then who knows what kinds of psychic bonds death creates?

I was going to drive to Bend to visit, but Kate's physical condition had stabilized and she was ready to be transferred to a rehab facility. Judy had been debating about whether to use a rehabilitation center in Portland or move her to a specialized placement out of state. She finally decided that, for now, it would be best to remain close to home. Kate was still incoherent and it would be weeks, even months, before we would know the extent of the brain damage.

As soon as Kate was settled into the facility in Portland, I went to see her. I was nervous driving to the hospital, not knowing what to expect. Because of my trip, I had not seen Judy since the day of the accident when I walked in her front door and told her that Kate was the one who had survived and Elana had died. Our very last contact was when she hugged me and whispered through her tears that we had one daughter between us now.

When I arrived, Kate was propped up in a hospital bed in a room filled with flowers and balloons. Two teddy bears were at her side. She was attempting to eat soup with her left hand. Her head was shaved, her arm and leg were in a cast, and a small row of stitches crossed her chin.

"Hi Katie, how are you honey."

Her smile was warm and the hug sweet, but she was struggling to recognize me. In a rote voice she said, "I was in an accident."

"Yes, honey, I know, but look how much better you are." She had been told she had been in an accident, but not about her father's or Elana's death. "It's so good to see you, I brought you some goodies, lotions to make your skin feel soft, special powder and a lipstick."

"Oh, thank you." There was a vacancy in her eyes as she spoke. She put the lipstick up to her nose and smelled it curiously.

"Put it on your lips like, this honey, and then look in the mirror." I felt as if I were talking to a six year-old.

Kate had no reference point about anything in her life. All she could do was respond to simple yes and no questions about the weather, hospital food, or visitors. She had no memory of anything before the plane crash. Everything she did was as if for the first time and it was hard to tell what clicked. She showed me her daily schedule of meetings with the physical therapist, speech thera-

pist and occupational therapist. Judy said they had to coax
her to concentrate, even for five minutes, on learning the
calendar or how to tell time.

Keeping Vigil

The next day, I arrived balancing three lattes from
the outside world. We laughed at the incongruity as we
sipped the hot froth and munched scones.   ·
"Do you want a sip of coffee, Kate? Do you remember
what a latte is?" I think we were all trying to be strong for
each other.
Judy, her mother, and her sister Dael kept vigil. Kate's
brother, Rian, took the semester off from college and was
there every day, doting on Kate like a mother hen. When
I walked in, he sat slumped in the chair, his blond salty
good looks barely recognizable under the strain. I looked
at him and thought, poor Rian, a sophomore at Tufts, suddenly summoned back from the sheltered environment of
academia to find his father dead and his sister in a coma,
his innocence and expectations of a bright future shattered. I bent over and gave him a big hug. The bond of our
shared grief made me feel closer to them than anyone else
I knew.
Judy couldn't even begin to process the loss of her
husband with Kate's life hanging so precariously in the
balance. I know her pain was doubled by mine, doubled
again because her husband was the pilot. She had never
been entirely comfortable with Stu's love of flying. Her
own father had died in the crash of a small plane twenty
years earlier. And now the worst thing imaginable had
happened. Her husband had gone down in a small plane,
leaving their daughter in critical condition and another
child dead. It was still all so unreal. I didn't know what
else to do but to be around them. Common fate bonds like
nothing else.

I went through the motions of daily activity in a trance. I had no investment in material concerns. I was indifferent to world affairs and politics. I desired absolutely nothing in this world other than having my daughter back.

I walked around with an enormous sense of compassion and caring for everyone and everything around me. I gravitated to the news of others who had suffered and was heartsick for them. I was kind and helpful to people on the street. I allowed others to go in front of me in busy supermarket lines. I didn't get angry at bad drivers who cut me off. I helped elderly and disabled people carry packages. My heart had been ripped open and in the rawness of my own pain, I felt an inexplicable and overwhelmingly powerful compassion for my fellow man.

Wherever I went, people opened their hearts to me. My utter vulnerability seemed to invite them in. I looked grief-stricken. I didn't try to cover it up with make-up or a facade of cheeriness. I had profound encounters with people who were just acquaintances, on street corners, in supermarkets. We would just start talking, riveted to each other's words, the traffic, shopping carts, and crowds ceasing to exist. They told me the about the losses in their own families, siblings who had died, grandparents who spoke to them through dreams.

There was so much love around me that this broken heart, bleeding and full of pain, was constantly being touched with love. I had no choice but to embrace it. It was a great paradox, the unfathomable anguish brought with it immeasurable love. The love everyone felt for Elana was linking us all.

One day when I came to visit Kate, Judy showed me the book she was keeping of Kate's progress. She looked at me rather intently and said that when Kate first emerged from coma and the endotracheal tube was removed, she frequently rambled about Elana and her father being in the "light." "What do you mean, in the light?" I asked.

"I don't know, it was the week she first regained consciousness and she was barely intelligible, but would say things like Elana is pure love, Elana is pure heart, she's light, she's in la la land, I want go to la la land with her."

"Oh my goodness," I said breathlessly, "Maybe Kate had a near-death experience."

Judy had kept a detailed diary of this early erratic communication in the hopes that a pattern of coherency could be detected. I asked if I could read it and curled up on the floor in the corner of the room. Each page had a series of disconnected phrases uttered from Kate's semi-comatose state when she first gained consciousness. The most remarkable were the ones about the accident and Elana.... *"Don't forget Elana, get the stretcher for Elana....Everyone's hurt that guy said it...What about those two no three...."* On another page, *"Oh Elana, what about the white picket fence houses that we won't be living in with our husbands and babies...what about our babies, oh no, Elana, what about our babies....Elana, we didn't plan this....Elana, are there babies where you are...my finger feels annexed, Elana help me."* This sense of loss was profound, especially given that Kate had no memory of the accident and had not been told anyone had died. Even more remarkable was Kate's repeated reference to Elana being in the "light" and how she wanted to be in the light with Elana. She'd mutter, *"Elana, you will become One— you will become heart...Elana has been struck as*

One...Elana is in the light. Elana's in....la la land. Daddy's in la la land....I want to go to la la land with them, I want to be with them...."

As I sat in the corner on the floor reading this, I was sure Kate had a near-death experience and had seen my daughter's soul ascend into the mysteries of grace. Despite the way a neurologist might interpret this disjointed discourse, I felt that Kate described some aspect of her father's and Elana's soul or life force moving toward the light at the time of the crash and that she herself experienced the pull between life and the light on the other side when she talked of wanting to go to "la la land." It seemed that in her semi-comatose state, she was able to remember what she had experienced at the time of the accident, even though she had no conscious knowledge of any of it. Even weeks later, when Judy told her that Elana and her father had died, she couldn't retain or comprehend this information, and when I would come to visit, she would ask how Elana was.

I finished the diary and closed my eyes. That my daughter might be in the "light" was deeply comforting. It soothed the unrelenting anguish I felt at not being with her in her last moments. I sat there pondering questions about the after death, questions I had never encountered before except perhaps in the abstract. What survives the death of the physical body? Is there a journey of the soul? Does consciousness survive, and, if so, as a personal identity? What did her last words, "I'm never coming home again," mean? Did Elana on some level know she was leaving? Was it her time? Is there such a thing as our "time?" Or was the plane crash a random accident, and she an innocent caught in human events? I thought about the bird screeching in the middle of the night, the strange behavior of the kitten, the butterfly at the funeral, and the birds on the beach in Portugal. Was she was trying to communicate with me?

Unexplained things which felt like signs from Elana occurred over the next week or two. One evening, I walked by her room and her desk lamp was on. I stood and stared at it, having no recollection of going into her room even as I obsessively retraced my steps. The next night, the desk lamp was on in my study when I hadn't been in there. Was I losing my mind, not remembering what I was doing, or were these signs? A few days later, I found my toothbrush lying in the sink in my bathroom. It had been a family joke that I didn't like Elana to use my toothbrush, which she would sometimes do anyway, often leaving the telltale mark of not putting it back. On another evening, I was getting into my car, feeling very sad and lonely after visiting old friends, and her driver's license was lying on my seat. Then, a guest who was taking a shower in the bathroom Elana usually used, found the words, *I love you* and a heart, drawn with a finger in the steam on the mirror. Who knows when Elana had done that. I had never seen it before.

It culminated the night my friend Diana stopped by the house while my literary agent, Natasha, was visiting. Diana and Elana had always had a special rapport. Elana was the child she didn't have, and Diana was the alluring mountain climber with her long blond hair, whom Elana idolized. We met when Elana was only four.

Conversation these days was uncommonly rich and we three women, all from such different backgrounds, sat over a bottle of wine talking. It was getting late, so I fixed some dinner and set a place for Elana because I knew she would want to be here. In the middle of dinner, when her absence was particularly felt, the chain on the front door began to rattle and sway. We all turned to look at it. There was a stillness and thickness in the air that made the hair on our arms stand up. No one said a word. It lasted less than a minute. We all knew that we weren't alone.

I had not been a religious person. I gave up any belief in God when I was in college. I certainly did not believe in a heaven or an afterlife. As much as I wanted to
think these strange occurrences were signs from Elana, I
looked for logical explanations. Did I not remember going
into the room and turning on the light? Was there a draft
or a large truck passing by causing the door chain to sway?
Did I get distracted and drop my toothbrush in the sink?
Was I reading an intent in what was just a random pattern of birds on the beach in Portugal? Did her driver's
license fall out of my purse? In my desperation, was I in-
terpreting events to satisfy my desires? I wanted absolute knowledge. I had to know, because if any part of
Elana's soul existed, then death had not snatched her completely beyond my reach.

I had a dream in which I went to be examined by a
psychiatrist to find out whether visions of Elana and signs
from her had been real. Just as the psychiatrist completed
the examination and was about to pronounce the answer,
he closed his eyes and fell asleep, and the dream ended.
Perhaps the dream was saying we cannot have certainty
about these things, one way or another.

Shortly after that dream, the signs stopped rather
distinctly. The sense of being in communion with her spirit
was gone. The house felt different. I would call to her and
there would be no signs. A new despair set in. No matter
how I cried, how I pleaded, how I prayed, the sense of her
proximity had changed and I couldn't call it back, I couldn't
will it back as if it was up to me. "Elana," I would cry, "all
I want is for you to check in occasionally, the way you
used to do when you were out with your friends." I felt
like she was abandoning me. I didn't understand what
had changed, or why. I felt betrayed. My tears were endless because now she was really gone.

PART II: Going Into the Deep
The Next 2 Months

The river of tears allows me on its banks,
but always I walk beside it.

I was somehow able to return to work seeing clients two days a week. This gave me a focus. My work took on a new depth. I had always felt vulnerable that as a therapist, if anything ever happened to Elana, grief would consume me and leave me unable to work with my clients, unable to earn a living. Now faced with my worse fear, I was surprised that I brought a deeper level of compassion and insight into my clients' losses and pain because of my own. A more profound sense of who they were opened to me as I sat there in my rawness.

The days I didn't go to the office, I often sat at my dining room table doing paperwork or responding to condolences. Everything I did took an exceedingly long time. Unable to concentrate, I'd get up and wander from room to room, roaming like a desolate animal in search of a lost cub.

There were boxes of tissue in every room. Alone in the house, the depths of despair could come upon me suddenly and without warning. Walking by the desk glancing at a photo, opening the refrigerator seeing the foods she loved, hearing her favorite music on the radio. Each image was like a knife in my heart opening a floodgate. Anguished tears raged through my body like a fire through a forest. They brought me to my knees, rolling over onto the hard ground, pounding the floor, moaning, sobbing, not caring about ever rising up again. My whole being felt as if it were about to shatter. I felt like I could disintegrate, that I could join death, and I didn't care. *I wanted to be with her.* This grief, so intensely physical, took me to the edge. It had no bounds. It felt like it had no end. It felt like it could swallow me. It almost did.

Oddly, it was a simple bodily need which kept me from going into the void after her. I'd be pulled out of this abyss because I became so congested that I couldn't breathe. I'd snap back to reality because I had to blow my nose. It was almost comical, nasal congestion, the internal regulator, the valve that kept me from joining death. For a year and a half it happened this way.

In time the intensity and frequency of these deep, dark tears diminished. I would remark that a day or two had passed without sobbing. But the grief in all its physicalness was always there, just under the surface. When it came, especially after I had begun to heal, it caught me by surprise. I would feel utterly abandoned by friends, angry at them for not calling, for not knowing how it still hurt.

The grieving for a child is a pain that separates you from everyone and everything. You may have caring and supportive friends who surround you, hold you up, love you, and cry with you and for you. But their lives return to normal. You alone live the unspeakable loss. No one else knows what it is like at the breaking point of the unbearable.

Anger and Rage

What was I to do with my anger? There was no one to blame. It was an accident that shouldn't have happened. We don't really know what happened, and probably never will. Chalked up to pilot error by the FAA, an altitude density miscalculation, a hot day at a high-altitude airport. But the pilot, a friend and a good man, was dead. His daughter was in a coma, his wife a widow. They were my neighbors; their daughter was Elana's childhood friend. How could I blame Stu?

I couldn't justify my anger because so many others have suffered tragedies worse than mine. Repeatedly, I talked myself out of it. One day shortly after the accident, a man came to do some carpentry repair at the house. He innocently asked about Elana's photo on the wall. I told him about the plane crash. His eyes welled up and he told me his eleven year-old son had died of leukemia. As he described the horrendous struggle with bone marrow transplants and the terror and pain his son endured, I felt enormously grateful that Elana didn't suffer. How could I be angry about the accident? Death was gentle to my child.

Everywhere I turned humanity bled. I watched Kurdish mothers wailing over mass graves as their babies died in their arms, and Bosnian children being blown up in the street. There are so many who lose children, children who suffer more than Elana had. What right did I have to rage? I am one of many. Perhaps it is the scream for us all that needs to be heard.

I knew it was there someplace inside, that rage that has no place to go. Just as in the first weeks following the accident I could be kind and compassionate to strangers, I soon found myself capable of being unnecessarily ungenerous to people on the street who were in my way. I would get angry at slow and stupid drivers, people in line at the espresso stand who asked to have every drink described after they had already had ten minutes in line to study the menu. Inside I wanted to scream, "Can't you see I've lost a child? Now get the hell out of my way!"

Lifelines

Each morning as the first rays of sunlight filtered through the forest canopy, I'd shuffle down the driveway through the wet leaves to get the mail. There was a chill in the air. The dew was untouched and shimmering. I'd pick up the newspaper carelessly thrown from the delivery truck, cross the street and open the mailbox, ever hopeful it would hold an answer to this pain. There was usually a note or card from an old friend, an acquaintance, a former client, one of Elana's friends or teachers, even from people I didn't know directly.

I saved every single card and letter about Elana, storing them in a white wicker basket on the old hatch cover table in my den. These cards were like a lifeline. I felt abandoned by the universe, betrayed by life's promise, alone with pain that threatened to swallow me alive. These cards penetrated the isolating nightmare, just for a moment. They helped me to hold on. Distant voices, bearing witness, reaching into my heart, holding me in the light. The tears that flowed as I read these notes were different from the anguished tears of missing Elana. These deep, rich tears, born of others' compassion and love, were healing.

When I felt most alone, I'd go to the basket and randomly pick a few cards. *We hold you in our hearts....Elana will always be the sweetest, most generous and most beautiful girl I have ever known....I will always love beautiful Elana and cherish her memory forever....We are heartbroken for you....I know if we all cried together, there wouldn't be enough tears....*

I would look at the images on the cards, many of which were extraordinary, aptly reflecting some part of Elana's spirit and the journey she has taken—a young woman riding on a flying horse over a mythic city into eternity, a young maiden in a garden of fairies and flowers, an Indian painting of birth and the circle of life. Mythic images telling me she is part of something bigger now, she is in a place I can't go.

Death is the ultimate abandonment and knowing that people care, and hearing how much your child is loved, hearing the stories and anecdotes keeps some part of your child alive. Knowing that I was held in a circle of love helped to keep me from going under at a time I was most vulnerable.

I'm Afraid I Will Forget

I'd come home from work, open the front door. Nothing in the house moved. I'd turn off the burglar alarm, throw my coat over the bannister and sink into a chair putting my feet up on the table. The emptiness had its own presence.

The way she lived inside me was slipping away. What if I forget what she sounded like, the scent of her signature fragrance, the way she plopped her book bag down in the middle of a floor marking her presence—*I have returned from school and am ready to be the center of the universe once more.* What if I forget how she moved through a room, the mischievous little smile, the way she groaned in exasperation at me, the way she could fall to her knees laughing at herself, the bemused look on her face when she tried to get something she wanted and knew she was stretching the point, so characteristic of the quintessential Elananess; the "mmm, mmm, this is yummy" when I made her favorite foods; the charming incantation that melted my resolve, "Mom, would you please make me and Erika a sandwich," the earnest urgency of "Mom, please, please can I borrow your turquoise earrings? I promise I won't take them off for PE. I won't let anything happen to them. You can trust me." The perennial "Mom, did you see my assignment book, math homework, blue sweater, soccer shoes; Mom, I can't fall asleep, I'm nervous about...." The intensity of adolescence sits itself in the middle of your life. Now it was gone and there was a disquiet in the house.

I could still remember these things, but I couldn't feel them as I did when she was here. Our mother-daughter dance, her animation, her smile, her delightfully unselfconscious sense of humor, even her pouting and snarling. They were not in my bones, they were not inside me anymore. As the weeks went by, my visceral sense of her diminished. She was slipping further and further away.

Time lessens grief by softening the edges of memory. I'm not sure this is a fair trade.

Walking down the hall, her room beckoned like a searchlight on a dark sea. I'd turn from where I was going and enter. I could not resist. Sometimes I'd just stand there. It all looked so different to me now, almost as if I were seeing it for the first time, almost as if I were seeing her for the first time.

I'd sit down on the floor and rummage through her desk drawers looking for a vestige, some part of her I hadn't known before. Finding a drawing or poem I had never seen was like finding a piece of her soul. I examined the contents of her box of mementos—letters from friends from camp, letters from her father while he lived in San Francisco, postcards from me when I traveled, notes passed back and forth between her friends at school as they struggled to work out their friendships, medals and ribbons from track and ski competitions, the draft of her speech when she ran for class president, her baby teeth, a book of sketches from an art class she took one summer in San Francisco—studies of her father's hands, a chair, a room upside down, a rose lying next to a woman's shoe, a self-portrait reflected in a mirror. When did she learn to draw so well?

One day, I came across a poem about death stuck in between two books. I vaguely remembered her writing it as part of an English assignment in the sixth or seventh grade. Whatever it was then, it meant something else now. Scrawled across a page strewn with drawings of flowers, angling downward at the end as if fading off, it read....

WHAT DOES IT MEAN TO DIE?

What does it mean to die?
Is your soul just lost in space
Or is it something else?

Do you come back to live
as you have always desired?
Is there another life in your imagination
that you can continue forever?

Does you soul stay on Earth
to go about living just as it has before?

Could it be that your body
disappears and you are swallowed
up into a world only to find
it is a world of nothing?

I suppose no one knows and
We must all wait and see

Except when the time comes
It is always too late

What does it, does it
Me
   e

       e

           e
               ean to die?

    I put the poem down and sat silently. These forays into her room were windows into her soul, a rare view unencumbered by maternal proprieties and projections. I could see her passion for travel and adventure, her creativity, her desire for excellence, her deep aesthetic sensitivity, her concern and distress about the environment, the deep connection to her friends, her determination and discipline as an athlete, her humor, her love of music, and a world view so like mine at her age. It was a welcome but startling revelation to see so many parts of myself reflected in my child and to see the gifts she had that were different than mine. I don't think I fully appreciated our likeness because I wanted her to be more than I was, not have my bad habits, fears, and limitations. Now I felt as if I had not only lost a daughter, but a soulmate.

Death gives us different eyes. It filters out the static and noise of everyday concerns. It lifts the veil of parental shoulds and expectations and reveals the utter marvel of a child's being. Death's gentle hand offers up a panoramic view of the soul's essence. Death allowed me to see close-up what was only a faint outline on the horizon. In some ways I came to know Elana better after she died.

Richard

Richard didn't know what to do, but he was always there for me. We had been together for three years. He couldn't fix my pain although there were times I felt he should have. What is wrong with him, I thought, can't he *do* something? Why doesn't he follow me into her room and say something to make it better? Why does he have so few words?

Those closest to you most feel your pain, while at the same time you expect them to be able to do more for you than they can. Often I had no patience for the problems of his day, his anxieties about work or his children. They seemed so inconsequential compared to what happened to me. I would think how could you let this bother you, at least you have your children.

I know I pushed him away. I had little left to give. He was probably as lost as I was, steeling himself against the rawness of my anguish as he had steeled himself against other losses in his own life, but I couldn't let him be who he was when I was so needy. When I'd wander around the house listless, unable to extricate myself from the grip of my grief, he would retreat. I felt betrayed. I'd rage inside, I'm the one who lost a child, I'm the one with a thunder-ing ache that silences me. How can you not know what to say? How can you not know how to help me? Why can't you be more like my women friends—they know how to offer comfort.

Intellectually, I understood he was doing the best he could. His face was drawn, his eyes red and tired. He'd look at me quizzically through his wired-rimmed glasses. I'd gaze back at him, the greying beard, the furrowed brow, remembering how his whole face used to light up when he smiled. There were many uncomfortable silences between us now.

My melancholy colored our relationship. Our time together could be lifeless. I was able to function better when other people were around. I wondered if I would ever be capable of truly loving again or being happy. Would he be able to stick it out? I was damaged merchandise now; it would diminish certain aspects of his life.

Painful Surrogate

On the weekends when Richard's children were with him, I went over to his house. I had always hoped to have a relationship with a man who had children close to Elana's age so that there could be a lively family atmosphere in our home. After twelve years of being a single parent, the dream I had waited for so long was gone.

Now I trudged up the front steps with a false cheeriness and dutifully walked inside. I listened to the news of the day while he prepared dinner and I made salad. The four of us sat at the dining room table with a spread of a rich Hungarian stew, fresh bread, and greens. This was Richard's earnest effort to create a sense of family life for his children out of the fragments of divorce.

Richard's son, Aaron, who was Elana's age, talked excitedly about the school play, upcoming track events and the college catalogues he'd been reading. I tried to listen but I was distracted. I couldn't look at him without thinking of Elana. What would she be doing in track if she were here. What colleges would she be thinking about? How would she have scored on the SAT? Comparing, why was I comparing, why couldn't I let it be? Elana, like most female adolescents, had matured earlier than Aaron; but now he was catching up, almost six feet tall, dark and good looking, filling out. He even had a girlfriend. Why couldn't I just be happy for Aaron without enviously wondering what Elana's achievements would have been? Why this constant comparison? On the outside, "Hey, you'll do fine in the 400 meter." On the inside, "I don't belong here, this is not the way it is supposed to be. I want to be back in my own house with my own child."

After dinner Dorothea, Richard's thirteen year-old daughter wanted to make plans to spend the night with her friend Caroline. This was all too familiar. Caroline and Dorothea, like Kate and Elana, or Liz and Elana, or Chessy and Elana, the requisite weekend sleep over arrangements, a ritual of female pubescent that I had experienced for years. Being with Dorothea wasn't as difficult as witnessing the life experiences Aaron was having that Elana would miss.

Deep sigh. Nothing to do but sigh. Life marches on without my daughter. Time to clean up from dinner, pick up Caroline, and head to the movies. I laugh at their jokes, try to engage with them. Going through the motions, always going through the motions. Burning inside...*I don't know if I can keep doing this. But then what would I do? I'd be all alone and would have no one.* No matter how I tried, I couldn't make it feel the way it used to. Elana's loss was a dark shadow over my relationship with Richard's children.

The Car

The car became a refuge from the social requirement to behave as if life didn't hurt. The tears could come suddenly out of nowhere while driving. On the way home from

54

work, the store, a movie, a friend's house, I'd find myself sobbing. All alone in that cushioned, well-appointed interior, where no one could see or hear, I could release the pain from having to witness the life I lost—teenagers pushing and teasing each other as school let out, toddlers grabbing for cookies in the grocery store, little girls in pigtails skipping down the street as Elana had. In the car, I was sealed off from it all.

Often, I'd pull into the driveway after a long day at work and not be able to get out of the car. I didn't want to go into the house and enter the half-life my world had become. I'd sit there staring at the porch light, immobilized. I didn't want to talk to Richard, I didn't want to be cheery for his children. I wanted to be with my grief, in my private womb, my private tomb, my car—where I could descend into the sorrow I held at bay all day.

I would lie across the front seat drifting back in time, thinking about Elana. The wonderful smell of new leather upholstery intensified my longing for her and the sadness I felt about the car. This was the new car I was supposed to enjoy, the reward for all the hard work on my first book. The car I postponed buying each year, holding out until Elana was ready to drive. The car I finally bought so that she could inherit the old blue Saab which she had lusted after since the eighth grade.

I hadn't seen anything that made Elana as happy as the fantasy that someday the rattling old Saab would be hers. It was her ticket to freedom. Humming and singing whenever she turned the ignition, her hair blowing in the wind, music loud, a big smile on her face, she was somewhere else. Everyone came to identify that blue Saab with Elana. For all her dreams, for all her waiting, she died three weeks after being given the keys. And my luxurious new car carries the memory of its predecessor. Some things you can't escape. Everything that mattered in my life had an association to Elana.

I visited Kate often in the rehab center. It became a new routine. I'd drive across the bridge to the east side of town, weave my way through the maze that is a modern day hospital campus, park in front of the small red brick building marked Legacy Rehabilitation Services, and walk down that long white corridor lined with wheelchairs. Teenagers who can't hold up their heads, parents with young children in body casts peering out of doorways— the hallway of uncertain futures.

Today Kate was propped up on the bed wearing a colorful lavender sweat suit. The bandages which had been on her hands to keep her from involuntarily picking her face had been removed and she was looking more like herself. She showed me all the cards and gifts she had received. Then, with a coy smile and a bashful glance, she uncovered a letter she had just finished writing to a boy she liked, a longtime friend, now in college. Scrawled sideways across a wide-ruled notebook page in the large uneven characters of a child just learning to write, were three short lines. It was a strange juxtaposition, the typical female adolescent delight in receiving attention from a boy and the letter she wrote back with the penmanship and content of a second grader. But this was progress. Kate was participating in her own healing now, proud of the little things she was learning to do.

A small wheelchair sat in the corner of her room. We helped her into it and went into the community room for her to eat dinner. Conversation with Kate still revolved around simple matters of the day. She could recognize her friends and now understood that Elana and her father had died.

Watching Kate come back from coma was like being part of a miracle. She was out of danger, but recovery from coma is a slow process. It is measured in seven stages of regaining neurological functioning, all very unpredictable.

It would be a long time before we knew if there was permanent brain damage. I don't know how Judy did it. She was there day and night. I was always relieved as I walked out of those swinging double doors into the cool night air. If this had been Elana, could I have handled it? The not knowing, seeing your child, once vibrant, now monosyllabic. I went home to a painful certainty. Judy lived with a painful uncertainty.

Lynn Osborne

The first time I heard the name "Osborne" it was with the relief that this faceless party didn't have anything to do with me or the plane Stu Moore was flying. A voice from the control tower, "There is a problem with a plane concerning an Osborne party, we don't have any details...." That combination of horror and relief, a faceless person down in a plane, not anyone you loved. But that did not turn out to be the case. Keith Osborne was the co-pilot.

I met Lynn Osborne, Keith's young widow, while visiting Kate in the rehab center. Her husband had been a flying buddy of Stu's. I'll never forget the shock of walking into the hospital room and being introduced to this sweet, innocent college girl with a blond pony tail who was sitting on Kate's bed. I almost wept when I saw her. She was just a child herself. She could have been my daughter, anyone's daughter. She got up and we hugged. "Oh, Lynn, I'm so sorry." I looked at her sad pale blue eyes, porcelain complexion, and delicately drawn lips—she was no longer a faceless name.

I sat on the bed with my arm around her feeling very maternal, "How are you doing, Lynn?" "Not very well. I can't eat or sleep, I can't even be alone in our apartment at night, I have to stay at my parents."

She opened a delicate gold locket which she wore around her neck and showed me Keith's picture. Blond wispy hair, clean cut, young and handsome. I had assumed

57

the co-pilot was a middle-aged man like Stu, especially because he was an instructor. Somehow that would have made the tragedy less. But Keith was only twenty-two. He and Lynn had been high school sweethearts, married less than a year. This plane stole the lives of two young people barely out of the nest.

Blind Dates

Your friends do it out of love. They tell you of someone you should call who has lost a child. They know their friend will be glad to talk to you. Sometimes they arrange a meeting, a walk, or coffee. Blind dates, I called them. Someone you might not ordinarily have had contact with except for losing a child. Two people thrown together by a caring friend. An introduction service you would never want to be part of, but you are and will continue to be, first as junior member, then as the mentor as friends ask you to talk with someone who has just lost a child.

I went on a few of them. It wasn't always the right chemistry. It felt awkward being with someone whom I didn't know sharing the most vulnerable, devastated part of myself. It worked better when it happened spontaneously, when I encountered people on my own who had lost children.

One time at a meeting of Compassionate Friends, a support group for bereaved parents, I was sitting next to a woman whose seventeen year-old daughter had just died in a car accident. As people in the group told their story, hers was the loss that resonated in every cell of my body. At the end of the meeting we talked. We told each other what our daughters were like, their goodness, brightness, and promise. Both of us single parents with very deep bonds with our girls, we understood the depth of the other's loss the way no one else could. It was uncanny, our daughters seemed so much alike, or maybe it is the way death allows us to see those we love. She told me about the hor-

58

rible accident, a head on collision, a car crossing the median strip. The boyfriend was driving. He survived, but her daughter was rushed to the hospital in critical condition. She sat at her bedside throughout the night holding her hand, praying. The next day, brief moments of hope, her eyes opened, then infection, spiraling fever, internal bleeding, and she slipped away. I told her about the plane crash, Elana's last words, and the mistaken identity. We were riveted by each other's story. Everything else was blocked out. There was only the love we felt for our daughters and the deep sorrow that was in our hearts. As we embraced and said goodbye, our eyes drenched with tears, all separateness dissolved. The feeling of love was so overwhelming that I felt at the highest level we were one, as if her wound became my wound and my wound became her wound. It was a moment of transcendence. Though we had barely met, and never saw each other again, it was one of the most profound encounters I have ever had. I was every mother who had lost her baby and my heart was as big as the world.

The Other Mothers

The mothers of Elana's friends did wondrous things. They planted poppies in my garden that surprised me in the spring. They took care of the house, the food, the arrangements, the other people at the time of the accident. They brought gifts of wine, flowers, casseroles. Like a reserve battalion they mobilized, synchronized, and marched through each day taking care of everything. Even when I was in Portugal, they silently and anonymously moved through my life. I came home to find hinges repaired, the tool shed cleaned, new dish towels neatly folded on the counter. They were angels in disguise.

I wanted to thank them and give them the gifts I had brought back from Portugal. I invited them all over for coffee. Judy couldn't be there, but I had other opportunities to give her a gift. As people arrived, there were the kind of hugs that don't let loose, the "How are you, it's so good to see you," spoken from the heart. This was no ordinary coffee klatch, we were convened by the fates. As we sipped our coffee and munched on scones, conversation was rarified. Quiet tears ran down my cheeks, I didn't have to hide how I felt with these women, "I don't know what I have left in life that matters. All I want is to find a way to still have a relationship with her. I don't care about anything else." We were all mothers of sixteen year-old girls. They all understood what it meant to lose a daughter. In response, others told their stories: one whose two younger brothers both drowned at the age of four, another whose mother had lost everything in a fire which destroyed the family home and killed her father, leaving them destitute. Moments of exquisite silence save for the voice of each woman as she shared her story. Life's fortunes rising and falling, one would never suspect looking at these successful women what had come before. I felt less alone in loss. We ended with hugs and kisses. Promises of having coffee again. We never did.

What else could they do? What else is there to do? I know they kept me in their hearts, but our lives intersected around our daughters. Our paths would no longer be crossing as they had for the last ten years at school functions, the track and soccer fields, or the ski bus. We had been part of a clan, mothers whose daughters were the same age, were classmates, or friends. Now I was no longer a member of that clan, no longer part of the camaraderie around school life. But I know that the loss of the daughter of the clan is something that will never be forgotten and I take comfort in that.

Running with Francie

There are only a few people who can truly be with you in your grief. They instinctively know how to comfort

60

and what to say. Sometimes your good friends don't know what to do after the immediate crisis has subsided. They can listen, they care, but they are afraid. Their words are kind, but you sense their discomfort and you try to protect them.

The person who was the most present and consistent source of comfort to me was not even a close friend. She was the mother of one of Elana's childhood friends, Chessy, who was with Elana on that last weekend in the mountains. We had seen our daughters grow from ribbons and giggles to determined young women. We had periodically run together, chatting and comparing notes about our girls. After the accident, we ran together almost every other day for a year. It was good for both of us, but it was a life preserver for me. We both instinctively understood what these runs were about. Elana's father went to the synagogue every morning that first year. He'd ask if I wanted to go. I'd always say, no thank you, I was going on a run with Francie.

Monday, Wednesday, Friday, and sometimes Saturday. A reason to get out of bed. I'd grab a glass of juice, pop a few vitamin C capsules, jump in the car and drive over to her house so we could do the Fairmont Loop—3.75 miles, mostly flat, the way we liked it best. "Ready, yeah, I'm ready. Let's go." Pounding the pavement, like molasses at first, then the rhythm carrying us effortlessly. An unsisterly competitiveness as we hit our stride, passing other women, glaring at their painted fingernails and perfectly coordinated jogging outfits. Some days wanting to take the shortcut and skip the hill, others pushing to finish in our best time. Catching up—her friend in the hospital who was dying, job searches, men, and always our girls.

Francie Stevenson was my witness, my mother, my fellow spiritual pilgrim. We ran in the crisp morning dew of early fall. We bundled for the cold, blustery winter chill. We greeted the freshness of spring rain as the cherry trees came into bloom, and we went deep into the forest in

61

summer's scorching heat. Always running no matter what, putting one foot in front of the other, moving through the cycles of the seasons, running and talking, running and crying, always about Elana. I didn't have to hide my grief, pretend I felt okay or make small talk.

Francie understood. My grief didn't frighten her. She lived with Chessy's pain. She could hold me and say, poor baby, as only one mother could say to another. I felt completely accepted and understood by her. We called each other honey. We loved each other's daughters. We became like girlfriends, like sisters. Goofy, silly, brave. Running with Francie sustained me through the worst of it. It softened the horrible loneliness of waking up to a house without Elana. It kept my body strong and nourished my spirit. Always after the runs with Francie, I felt as if I could get through the day.

Running, a modern amulet, like wearing a wreath of garlic or making the sign of the cross, warding off life's assaults so they don't settle in the bones.

Ivan

Ivan, Elana's father, called me every day. He was worried about me. It's not fair, I thought. We had worked so hard all these years keeping Elana a priority, trying to minimize the impact of the divorce on her. We did the right things as divorced parents, despite our ups and downs. Now every phone call, every "How are you?" ends in tears. The truth of the matter was that Elana's father was the only other person with whom I could share this grief. We were partners in sorrow, and for the first time in over a decade, we opened our hearts to each other.

Because Ivan is an attorney, he responded to most of the legal matters with regard to the insurance claims. Still, I had to be involved in decisions about how to proceed. Dressed in navy blue suits, we met in the lobby of the First Interstate Bank Tower and headed up to the twenty-fifth floor to see one of the top attorneys in aviation law. We were led into a corner office with a spectacular 180-degree view of the city and the snow-peaked Cascade mountains in the distance. The secretary motioned for us to be seated in two shiny leather chairs across from an imposing mahogany desk. I couldn't help but notice the photo of the attorney's wife and children in a small silver frame next to his files. Ivan had already been discussing the case with him, all undoubtedly very lawyerly, but now he was looking into the face of a mother who had lost her only child. He greeted me with warmth and spoke with compassion. "We may never know what happened. We're waiting for the FAA report, but their investigation won't necessarily uncover the cause of the crash. With a private plane, you have to prove gross negligence, not just negligence. There were probably problems with the weight of the plane and the altitude density calculation because it was a hot day and the airport was at 4,000 feet." Composed, solemn, I said I would never sue the pilot's estate. Everyone needed to understand that. We were friends.

He continued on about various options. It was hard for me to concentrate on the legal technicalities. My stomach hurt. Without realizing it, I was staring at Ivan. So much history in a face. It was hard to believe we had known each other for 25 years, harder still to think that this was the wild man in cowboy boots I met at a college hootenanny when the Sixties' promise and hopeful optimism shaped expectations of the future. Now, graying around the temples, wearing horn-rimmed glasses, stylishly dressed, still too youthful to be distinguished, he was a successful businessman. We had been married for ten years before we split up, but because of his move to San Francisco when Elana was only four, there was never an opportunity to enjoy her achievements together. And now look where we were. Damn it. We should be sitting in a tiny crowded office with no windows pouring over college catalogues with the school counselor, not in a fancy lawyer's office with thick manila files containing insurance investigation reports. This isn't what we signed up for.

The lawyer broke into my reverie, "The plane carried relatively little insurance and it has to be split four ways. There is another umbrella policy which the insurance company is now claiming contains an exclusion for operating an aircraft. It's worth taking them on. I think we have a chance. All parties, including the family, would stand to benefit." Closing my eyes, wanting to make this go away,

"Okay, do that. I just want to get out of here."

Dazed, out on the street. A teary hug, *oh Ivan*. Here with the man with whom I spent my youth. Is this how it all will end? Ivan rushing back to his office. Where did I park the car? Distracted, what should I do? What does money mean to me now? She's gone.

Tonic for a Broken Heart

The ritual was always the same, "Hello, little babies." They rubbed up against my leg, rolled over in the dirt and licked my hand in concurrence that their mother was home. No matter how sad I'd be feeling, no matter how lifeless and dispirited as I trudged up the driveway, the greeting of these three furry beings always warmed me and brought a smile to my face. My cats could disrupt the rising tide of my grief in an instant. I had no choice but to love them back and it dissolved the cloud that had followed me home.

I don't think of my three Himalayan cats as surrogate children, although they were groomed to be before Elana died. I got the cats and even started to breed them in anticipation of Elana graduating from high school and leaving home. Now, they *are* my babies, they know it and I know it. They absorb, deflect, and counter my sadness with nothing more than their presence. They evoke no painful memories. They are pure unconditional love presenting themselves to me in my darkest moments, luring me out of the depths with their soft white fur. Can it be more simple than that?

There were days when I would wander into Elana's room and lie across her bed. As the tears came so did China Cat, the kitten named by Elana, the one kitten I refused to sell after she died. She'd saunter in the bedroom and jump on the bed with a little mew. I clutched her like a teddy bear. Oh China, what are we to do? Burying my face in her neck, pouring out my saddest thoughts, my most regressed and vituperative impulses, my utter longing and fantasy about Elana's return, thinking...who else can I talk to like this?

I have no shame when it comes to my behavior toward my cats. I cradle them in my arms like a newborn. I find myself rocking them, rubbing noses and cooing when no one is around. When they roll over on their backs, I hold their paws and engage in a crude game of patty cake. I indulge in every form of stupidity without reserve. I give them my all. I think our pets draw on a direct line from our hearts when our love has no place else to go. They are unconditional love as you walk in the door, a good tonic for a broken heart.

I Couldn't Save Her

I ached that she died alone. Over and over I replayed how I saw her last moments. Waving to Chessy and Liz on the ground, warmed by a weekend in the mountains with her closest childhood friends, a tinge of excitement as the plane soared into the air, the beautiful timbered green of Eastern Oregon angling below, and seconds later clutching Kate's hand screaming....

I said to myself if I had been there, I could have saved her. On some level, I believed I could have. Perhaps it was just the projection of the power of a mother's love, but I could feel that power in every cell of my body. It was a

65

supernatural force field that could hold life. I knew she would have held on if I had been there. The fact is that Kate was the only one with a pulse when the Life Flight helicopter arrived minutes after the plane hit the ground.

That my child met death alone was a source of deep anguish. I had failed to protect my baby. I couldn't save her. I wasn't there at the end. She died by herself. What is there worse than that? I suffered because of what I imagined was her suffering. I suffered because of the limitations of human will. I suffered because I made the wrong decision and allowed her to fly in a private plane.

The guilt I felt about my failure to protect Elana was absolutely primal. It racked my soul and no amount of comfort or rationality took it away. In losing a child who was still under my protective mantle, I felt that *I* literally lost her; I was holding her hand, turned away for a moment, and she was gone forever.

The only comfort I had was knowing that Elana's body was tended by the Hevra Kadisha, an ancient Jewish order of women who ritually cleanse and pray over the body. I hadn't known about them, but the rabbi explained that it is an honored group of women whose identities are never disclosed and who ceremoniously prepare a body for burial. When he told me about what they did, I desperately wanted to thank them personally. They were with Elana in the most sacred moments after she died when I wasn't. They held her and cared for her when I couldn't. I beseeched the rabbi, please let me speak to them, can't you make an exception, they held my baby, they saw her bruises, they washed the blood from her face...please...please.... But it was forbidden. That these women lovingly and anonymously cared for my child, soothed her, bathed her, and said prayers for her at a time the soul is thought to be near the body, was a blessing for which I will be forever grateful. I stand in awe of these women whom I will never know or be able to thank.

Three weeks before the plane crash, I had sent the completed manuscript for my book on divorce to the publisher. It was a moment of exhilaration and relief. I had spent the summer working the final editorial revisions day and night after a terrible computer mishap. When my hard drive crashed, taking with it hundreds of hours of rewriting, I felt defeated. I remember nervously waiting for the reports from the data retrieval specialist, optimistic at first—90 per cent chance of retrieval, the prognosis worsening as they got further into the hard drive. The final report—terminal, all data lost, hard drive dead.

I felt I didn't have it in me to do the revisions all over again. Finally I had to say to myself, this is just work, it is not cancer, it is not a human life, my daughter is fine, it is not the end of the world. I was able to get back to work, and chapter by chapter did the revisions all over again. It took my entire summer. I was very conscious of there being few summers left before Elana would be going off to college, and now I had lost this one. I didn't even have time to go shopping with her or take her to the beach. I breathed a huge sigh of relief the day I put the manuscript in the mail. Finally free, I could relax and catch up with Elana, make up for the summer. The plane crashed three weeks later. This was the end of the world.

The book remained. I had to deal with it. I had to contend with deadlines, proof reading the galleys, indexes and other production details. As much as I found the demands of the book's publication and publicity difficult, I think the book kept me from giving in to my desire to put my head down and go to sleep forever. On one level I didn't care about the book, on another level I cared very much. It was three years of effort in between earning a living and taking care of a child. As broken as I was, I must have understood I couldn't abandon my book because it was the only thing I could see left of my future. Looking back, I think the void left by Elana's death would have consumed me had it not been for the book.

Elana never got to see the book published. She wasn't there to share my childlike excitement the day the book jacket arrived with my photo on the back. Her presence was sorely missed at the book signing party. She didn't get to share in any of the recognition that comes from having a mother whose first book is published. All my joy was tempered by her not being there to share in it. She deserved to be part of it. She put up with me writing every spare minute for two years. And the book, the result of twenty years of experience as a therapist and divorce mediator, became a culmination point professionally, rather than a jumping off point. All my ambition died with my daughter and I didn't care.

A New Definition of Normal

I was having lunch in a small café with one of my oldest and dearest friends. "Julie, I will never be normal again. Not only have I lost my daughter, I've lost myself. I am an aberration of a former self, a half self, a mutant. I'm afraid I'll never have my old self back. I don't know who I am anymore. I feel like I'm adrift, being carried further and further away from the shore. I see the distant bank, but I know I can't go back. What am I going to do?"

With the penetration that comes from looking truth in the eye and the trust of twenty years of friendship, she said, "You have to find a new definition of normal." For the very first time it hit me: I would *never* be the person I was before Elana's death.

I didn't realize how much being a mother was at the core of my existence. I didn't realize all the little ways my life was structured and organized around Elana, from feeding, nurturing, transporting and protecting, to cheering, motivating, watching, witnessing, advising, listening, worrying, and loving more than life itself. The acts of motherhood become deeply embedded in the psyche and create neurological pathways that automatically and without consciousness reach into and pilot every part of your life. I thought I had created a Nineties' balance between parenthood, career, and relationship. As far as I am concerned, that balance only exists as a sociological construct. Maternal instincts and behavior are biological. A part of you is ripped out when a child dies, regardless of your other children. There is a never-to-be-filled hole.

A new normal, I thought. Does this mean pain is always with me? Will I be permanently gripped in this existential nightmare? Do I lower the ceiling of life's expectations forever? I am a grieving parent now, an unsolicited member of the "club," as my friend Loretta called it. This is my new self-definition. To see oneself as a grieving parent is better than not seeing oneself as a parent at all.

Losing your child defines you for a long time, maybe forever. In the beginning it is the most powerful emotional and spiritual force in your life. You only think of yourself as someone who has lost a child; other aspects of your identity pale and lose their emotional resonance. Even when a familiar rhythm in your life returns, I don't think the old feeling about yourself ever completely returns. You are fundamentally dismembered by the death of a child and as you try to reclaim parts of yourself, scattered you know not where, they do not fit back together in the same way. Julie was right, I think you do have to find a new definition of normal.

Reunions

She'd come running to me, jump into my arms, legs straddled around my waist, hang onto my neck and rest her head on my shoulder. *Oh, Elana, how I love you.* A drink of ambrosia, to be holding her again. A long, delicious hug like those that went before. Deepened by absence, intensified by longing, these hugs, the ephemeral reunion of a mother and child. And they came to me only in dreams. I'd lie there stunned, unwilling to move in the aftermath of the palpable sweetness of her embrace, a reality far more wanted than one waking hour of the life I had. I turned to Richard, "I think Elana's spirit came to me in a dream last night. It wasn't an ordinary dream. She was about five and jumped in my arms the way she used to when I picked her up from the babysitter after work. All she did was hug me and hold on tight. It was strange, unlike other dreams about Elana, where she is a character or part of events. I have no other words except to say she was a presence."

I have had this type of dream two or three times since Elana's death. I call them visitations and puzzle over them because they are different from any dream I have ever had. Always the experience of the embrace, visceral and immediate, has the adoring quality of the love a young child has for its mother, the love that Elana and I once had. In the dreams, I always know she cannot stay, I always know she has been away in a place that I cannot understand, but the intensity of the loving embrace feels like a palpable presence, beyond the stirring of my unconscious wishes and desires. She comes back to love me. There is no other message, nothing else really happens. *I want to hold you forever*, I would say, but the dream would end. I'd awake joyful for the experience, but missing her more. It was an unearthly contrast, in a split second, the forces of consciousness bringing me back from a dimension outside of time which I wanted to remain in forever.

What Would Elana Want Me To Do?

Lying in bed late at night, aching for her, a thick impenetrable emptiness engulfs me. It is bigger than the room. There is no way through it. I curl up into a ball. A feeble exhale...there is no reason to go on...what is the point...what matters to me now.

I don't think about Richard, my friends or family. Staring vacantly at the wall, I think about leaving this world. I wonder how I would do it. But then a voice intrudes, "*Elana would be angry if you ended your life. She wants you to be happy, she doesn't want you to give up on life because of her.*" Damn it Elana, I don't want to be here if you're not.

I roll onto my back. Reason takes over. I put myself in her place. I imagine my last days, holding her hand, telling her that this is my time, not hers, how important it is for her to have a full life. I would beseech her to live her life more for my love, not less for my absence. I see how sad and angry I would be if she let my death destroy her. If this was how I felt, I knew she would want the same for me.

As time went on, it became like a mantra—Elana wants you to be happy, she doesn't want you to be suffering, she wants you to remember her life with joy. Whether I was driving home from work and couldn't get out of the car, listlessly going on a bike ride or a hike just to get through a Saturday afternoon, I'd say to myself, "She wants you to heal, she wants you to go on living." I'd take a deep breath and have a just a little more energy to face what I had to. I did this to honor her memory, not because it is what my pain wanted of me, but what *she* would want of me. I did it because if I left this world first and left her behind, more than absolutely anything, I would not want her to suffer. I would not want her to give up on life.

The Only Way out Is up

We are compelled by our pain to seek the answers suffering asks. I was having tea with the mother of one of Elana's friends who had lost a daughter in a tragic mountaineering accident. Sitting in her sunlit solarium, she put her arms around me in friendship and love. She said that all she wanted to do when her daughter died was to survive. She recalled her own mother who after the loss of her young husband gave up trying to raise her four children and died within two years of the death of her husband. It became very important for my friend simply to make it through each day and go on living and not abandon her own family, as she felt her mother had.

I sat there, sipping the tea, thinking—survival, was this all I could hope for, living with death by your side, unmastered, unhealed, internal bleeding. I was deeply touched by the integrity of her story, but for me survival as an ultimate goal carried an image of constant pain. I could not imagine simply picking up the threads of my life, getting over Elana's death, and moving on. I knew I had to incorporate her death into my life to give it new meaning, otherwise too much of me would die with her.

With startling clarity, I saw that Elana would be a greater teacher in death than she was in life. I thought there are three ways a person deals with devastating loss; either you give up and on some level remain a victim of your fate, or you simply try to survive and go on, or the pain which cracks you open becomes your teacher. You are willing to follow it where it takes you, bow to it, be led into the unknown. It chews you up and spits you out a different person. Eventually it gives you the gift of serving others. I didn't know how to do this or even what it meant. All I knew was that this was the path *I* had to take. Somehow, I had to transcend this loss. That was my only starting point.

I had to find a way to honor Elana's death through the things I did in my own life. I thought, if I could bring joy into the world, if I could help other children, if I could help other grieving parents, if I could work with AIDS patients, if I could...if I could...if I could...but I couldn't make myself find a structure to do any of these things, nor did I have the emotional energy. Perhaps it was enough that I would allow the pain to lead me deeper into life. I would not try to shut it out.

"I'm Never Coming Home Again"

Elana's last words were a fire in my belly. I repeatedly replayed the scene: driving to Liz's house, Elana subdued and fiddling with the radio still irritated at my refusal to let her drive to the mountains herself; going inside, chatting with Liz's parents at the kitchen counter as the girls got ready; calling her over to say goodbye as she and Liz were leaving to pick up Chessy; hugging, saying I love you to each other; then out of the blue, snide, cool, unnerving, "I'm never coming home again." Not with the pitch of a petulant child, not with the authority of an adult; odd, slightly out of character, slightly out of context. "I'm never coming home again," her very last words, whispered in the midst of a hasty hug as she picked up her bags and walked out the door.

Everywhere I went, I told the story, querying friends if they thought her words were an insolent adolescent or a premonition. "Did something come through her? Was it her time? Is there such a thing as our time? Was she an innocent caught in the randomness of human events? And what does it mean if it was a precognition? Why do some people foresee their deaths?"

The responses were divided, "Teenagers are always threatening to run away or not come home, it was just a coincidence, she was in a huffy mood." Others looked me right in the eye as if they saw a deep and chilling truth, "on some level she knew and was telling you."

As if there was someone who would have absolute knowledge, with utmost sincerity, I kept asking. I had to make peace with whether I should have taken action. Should I have forbidden her to fly instead of quieting the anxiety her remark generated? Could I have magically undone the potency of her words by saying, "Don't say something mean like that when you are leaving for the weekend." Damn, why didn't I hear her words as a warning? Why did I have to be so rational? I didn't know if I would ever be able to forgive myself.

I played it every way in my mind. If I hadn't let her fly home, the plane would have been lighter and might not have had the problems gaining altitude, but then my refusal to let her fly would have been perceived as an overreaction. On the other hand, Lynn Osborne, the co-pilot's wife, said she would have gone along for the ride in Elana's place, so the plane's weight would have remained the same.

Of course, my friends all said I did nothing wrong. Had they been in my place they would have let their child fly. It was a short easy trip. But I knew her last words unsettled them also. I had been reading accounts of bereaved parents' experiences of their child's death which couldn't be explained by science; either some indication that the child knew he or she was going to die, or a message or sign from the child afterward. This only fed my need to know—did I fail to heed a cosmic warning or were her words just a horrific coincidence? And most importantly, the question which was now becoming a driving force in my life, does her soul or consciousness exist somewhere out there in eternity? The shock was wearing off. I was grasping for some meaning in her death.

The Quest to Understand the After Death

I started reading. I spent rainy afternoons when I didn't know what to do with myself tucked away in a dusty corner of Powell's Books flipping through the sections on metaphysics, quantum theory, eastern religion, mystic and esoteric traditions, and whatever scientific literature I could find on the survival of consciousness. I went to the library, sat at the computer, entered topic search, and typed DEATH.

When every parent's nightmare became the reality of my life, I could not tolerate it. I refused to accept death as having the finality I had always assumed. I remembered having said to myself in the midst of one of those parental anxiety attacks after reading about a horrible automobile accident in which three teenagers died, that if anything ever happened to Elana, I would have to believe in reincarnation. She had just gotten her driver's permit and this was a quick and unreasoned response to allay my anxiety. I didn't believe in God, in heaven, in an afterlife, let alone reincarnation. Yet I instinctively felt that the only way to survive the most unthinkable of all losses was not to accept death as an absolute and permanent end of all things. I knew I would be willing to completely change my beliefs if anything ever happened to Elana.

I heard myself telling friends that my relationship with Elana had ended in the physical world, but that it would continue to grow and change on a spiritual plane just as their relationship with their children would grow and change over time. I had no idea what I meant by this, except somewhere inside, I knew it to be true. I had no intention of abandoning a relationship with my daughter just because her time on the physical plane had ended. I would somehow find a way of remaining in contact with her.

I embarked on a study of Shamanism, an ancient method of altering consciousness for the purposes of healing and deriving spiritual knowledge. This had been a long-standing interest because of what I saw as parallels in the trance states to clinical hypnosis which I used in my work as a therapist. But now, I was drawn to the mysteries of the spirit world. I wanted to experience the realms which we cannot easily perceive through our analytic process or ordinary states of consciousness. I had to know whether there was more out there. I had to know the destiny of souls. I had to communicate with my daughter.

Elana age 3, and Mom

Elana, age 13, and Mom,
8ᵗʰ grade graduation

Slalom competition,
sophomore year

Forever Sixteen

Kate, Chessy, Erika, Elana
the last summer together, age 16

Chessy, Liz, Elana, Kate
Black Butte ranch, the day before the accident

PART III: The Questions and the Quest

Mexico

It started with a decision to attend a retreat in Mexico to study the Shamanic and spiritual practices of the Huichol Indians, who are called the Healing People in their own language and who remain one of the few intact pre-Columbian cultures. I would be gone over Thanksgiving, which was a plus because I dreaded the holiday without Elana and a taco instead of turkey sounded just fine. I was using the money that was in Elana's college account. This money represented the future Elana would never have and it felt absolutely sacred to me. It would be used only for high purposes—for helping others, for healing my broken life, not for the new roof or driveway repairs. So off I went to Mexico barely two months after the accident, not knowing exactly what I was looking for except that I had to move toward something.

I arrived in Puerto Vallarta amidst the traffic, diesel fumes, and midday heat. Eventually a van met me at the airport and we made our way through the maze of cars, hawkers, and souvenir stands, driving past a seemingly endless row of high-rise hotels. I breathed easier as the polluted hustle became a faint image in the rear view mirror. We turned off the main road toward a lovely hacienda on an unpopulated beach about 15 miles outside of town. Away from the crowds and noise, away from the grief that hung over my house, I buried my toes in the wet sand and let the salty breeze fill my lungs. Orange tile roofs peered out of the dense tropical foliage framing a scorched white beach. The surf lapped gently at my feet. The welcoming embrace of a tropical sun beat down on my back and the line where sea and sky meet beckoned as if out of a dream. Yes, being by the sea in a simple village was a good place to take my tears.

I milled about before dinner-time chatting with the other participants. Many seemed to be involved in some sort of Eastern spiritual practice or healing work. They spoke of various Buddhist teachers, dances for universal peace, aromatherapies and herbal remedies. One woman brought a twenty-five pound crystal. I wondered what I was getting myself into. I hoped this wasn't some New Age hokus pokus.

In the morning, we gathered in a circle under the outstretched limbs of a huge banyan tree. A prayer feather was ceremoniously passed around the circle as each person spoke about his or her intention in being there. The feather engendered a feeling of sacredness, dissolving the props of the ego. People spoke from the heart, expressing their desire for right-minded action, peace, and healing the earth. It was quite powerful, unlike any other gathering I had attended. As the feather came closer to me, my heart quickened. Should I reveal Elana's accident or quietly and privately deal with my pain? Did I have a responsibility to protect others and not burden them with what stirs abject terror? I worried that people wouldn't know how to treat me, that I would be a toxin in their midst. When the feather was placed into my hands, seized by the truth, barely able to speak, I humbly stated that I had lost my only child in a plane crash two months ago and prayed for healing for myself and all others who have experienced a shattering loss.

This was the beginning for me of understanding the depth of compassion that comes from community if you are open. Allowing myself to be vulnerable with people I didn't know was uncomfortable. But I had been stripped to the bone and I couldn't do much else but be there in my rawness. During the week, many people reached out to me. They weren't afraid of me. I was afraid of them.

Each morning we gathered in a circle under the sweeping branches of the ancient banyan tree. We learned about what the Huichol refer to as Nerika, an opening of the heart, the doorway to the sacredness of all creation, to the realms of the divine. I kept asking our teacher, "What do you mean a doorway, what realms of the divine? I don't understand how to do it." I couldn't even fathom the concept of Nerika so central to these people. He said you have to learn to see with your heart. You must learn to live in sacred relationship to all living things and honor the earth, our mother. These are the teachings of the Huichol people.

Go down to the beach and call to the four cardinal directions and ask each to guide you. Ask the wind to answer your prayers. Everything has a life force and spirit which will speak if you are willing to listen. Soon I was sitting in the hot sand, first facing east, shaking a rattle near my ear. I didn't understand what I was doing but said the words, "Oh, spirit of the east please help me for I am so lost." I waited and listened with my eyes closed, not moving a muscle, save shaking the gourd rattle I held in my hand. Nothing happened. I turned to the west sitting as still as I could, listening as hard as I could. I heard nothing, except the sound of my stomach rumbling. I turned to the north and south and continued rattling rhythmically with my eyes closed. What is supposed to happen? I don't hear anything. I looked up and saw scattered bodies hunched over rattles across a stretch of uninhabited pearl white beach. An odd sight. Closing my eyes, rattling, one last try. Something about patience and unfolding came into my mind; but I was too much of a novice to pay attention, let alone hear it as an ethereal response to my question. When we returned to the circle, others spoke of near mystical experiences and profound messages. I didn't get it.

Go down to the ocean and learn the language of the

ancient one, the sea, the giver of all life. Make an offering of chocolate in our tradition as you pray, and then dive under the water. Do this three times.

Soon, I was standing knee deep in the warm salt water vacantly staring at the gentle rolling of the waves. The setting sun cast a pink hue across the sky. I had an urge to eat the chocolate I held in my hand. Suddenly without thought, I reached up and threw the wafer out into the water as far as I could, crying aloud as I dove under the surf— "I pray for healing, I pray for guidance, I pray for Elana." Not knowing who or what I was calling to, but desperately wanting my prayers answered, I sank beneath the sea. Touching bottom, grains of sand falling through my fingers, I cast about the ocean floor like a creature before time. I reached the surface with a rush, stood up and twice more repeated my prayer. Each time I made my offering, I dove into the vast underneath, surrendering to the mystery of the deep, primal and rapturous. When I rose to the surface the last time, I lay on my back barely moving my arms. Looking up at the darkening sky and new crescent moon, I felt oddly renewed.

A Huichol Prayer for Elana

There are tears that hurt and tears that heal, tears that rip you open and tears that close the wound ever so slightly. I received such a gift at the close of the retreat when Brant Secunda, the leader, offered a special prayer to help Elana's soul on its journey. I understood from the anthropological literature that Shamans did what was called "psychopomp", meaning that they assisted the soul to cross over to the other side and ascend on its path. I wasn't sure I was ready for her spirit, soul, whatever you want to call it, to be ushered further into the vast unknowable. But as a mother I thought that if there is something on the other side, if she exists as consciousness, I couldn't deny her help from someone who apparently had supernatural gifts.

When Brant came to me in the circle, he closed his eyes and began singing a beautiful Huichol prayer while waving his prayer feathers in a circular motion. The singing intensified and his face took on an otherworldly quality. The chant was haunting, a powerful invocation entering into every cell of my body. I could feel that he was honoring Elana and appealing to the powers beyond on her behalf. Over and over he soulfully chanted her name. I began to weep in gratitude for the help my daughter was receiving when I felt so helpless to do anything for her. My knees buckled, gratitude gave way to lament..."*Oh my poor baby, my poor, poor baby.*" Brant took my hand, holding me steady. His entire body was vibrating as if a current were moving through him. My own body began to vibrate as he held my hand and sang these ancient prayers for Elana's soul. I lost all sense of time and space. The air became thick and still and I felt as if my heart had been lifted right out of my chest cavity and carried to the gods.

Miracles

There are people you meet on a journey of the heart who unknowingly move you from a familiar assemblage point. My roommate at the retreat was such a person. She was a nurse practitioner who had been trained in Touch for Health, a hands-on healing method that some hospitals use to reduce the effects of trauma and to aid post-operative recovery. She told me incredible stories about how moving energy with one's hands over patients without touching them could reduce blood pressure, bleeding, and signs of trauma. This was a world beyond me.

Late one night we sat across from each other on the edge of our beds, pictures of Elana that I had shared with her lying on the night stand between us. We sat in the stunned silence that follows the reality of seeing pictures of a child in her vibrancy and promise, no longer an abstraction, no longer just someone's daughter, but the little girl catching snowflakes in her mouth, playing in the bushes in a pink tutu, and whizzing down a snow-capped mountain.

In the almost transcendent awareness of what it means to be with someone whose sixteen year- old daughter's life was wiped out in a split second, while your own sixteen year-old daughter is safe at home, she said "I will tell you the story of what happened with the birth of my daughter." Haltingly, her dark eyes drifting inward, her torso stiff and straight, the only sound the rustle of curtains as the warm tropical breeze wafted through our room, she said, "This is a story very few people know." Something about the way she spoke sent shivers down my spine. I stared at her dark beauty, the chiseled features set off by hair pulled back into a pony tail, and waited. She took a drink of water, slowly put the glass back on the table and began.

"My sixteen year-old daughter was born with a rare and fatal condition for which there was no treatment. The baby was immediately taken from me and rushed by life flight helicopter to a pediatric medical center and put into intensive care. All through the pregnancy, I had the sense that my deceased grandfather was with me, watching over me, protecting me, telling me everything would be all right. But shortly before the due date, I had unnerving dreams that something terrible would happen with the birth. And it did. The baby was in intensive care for three days and failing, and there was nothing that could be done. People were trying to prepare me for the baby dying. But something in those dreams seemed to say that ultimately the baby would all right. I insisted she wouldn't die and I even told the staff that she would leave the hospital the next day. Everyone thought I was crazy, a bereft mother who had lost her senses. I don't know why I felt so strongly; I was unshakable. That evening, I was alone with the baby.

I took her little foot, holding it tightly and prayed from the bottom of my heart. I felt my grandfather's presence again and asked if he had it within his power to help. I prayed deeply, singularly, for the longest time. The next day I went to the nursery. The doctors and nurses huddled around the crib. Terrified that my daughter had died, I pushed my way through the crowd to see a pink cooing face, oxygen tubes dismantled. Miraculously, the baby's vital signs and color had dramatically improved and it appeared that she was going to survive. The hospital staff stood in disbelief. Doctors from other departments were invited to look at this child. No one had ever heard of an infant spontaneously recovering from this condition. I took her home the next day."

I sat spellbound. This was one of those stories that just stays with you and you don't know why. It took hold of something inside me. Perhaps I was hoping for some sort of miracle with Elana, that she might be watching over me and could help me as my roommate's grandfather had watched over her. When you lose a child, you want to believe in miracles.

Pilgrim

For seven days we were taught the spiritual and sacred practices of the Huichol. We made prayer sticks and offered them to Grandmother Ocean. Each evening, we danced the deer ceremony honoring the Huichol people's gods. We told Grandfather Fire our dreams and ritually cleansed in the sea. It didn't matter that these were not my traditions. It didn't matter that these rituals were based on tribal beliefs, a world view quite different from my own. They spoke to the utter isolation of my suffering. They gave me a venue to express my grief that didn't exist in my own culture. They gave me a way to connect with the wisdom of the ages. I danced and I sang my tears. My pain moved through me like the ebb and flow of the ocean's waves as the power of the *Tatamare*, the sun, warmed the frozen wasteland within. At the same time, there was a little voice inside that said, "What the hell are you doing, dancing for a deer spirit? This is nuts." Jolted back to ordinary reality, the full spectrum of my loss would return.

This was my first spiritual retreat. I didn't understand what I was supposed to get out of it. Answers, hope, release from pain? Did I think I would be better by the time it was over? Even though there were moments when I experienced the awe and power of the universe, I really didn't understand what it was or what it meant. At the end, I still hurt, I had no answers. People talked of seeing spirits, jaguar, deer, listening to the wind, being healed by the fire. I didn't get it. I was an absolute neophyte. I had no spiritual relationship to the natural elements, I couldn't hear the voices of the animal powers. The trees didn't speak to me. My stomach ached. I was tired of vegetarian food. I cried for Elana as much as ever. I participated without understanding, without knowing why, except that I *had* to do it. That these practices seemed to ease my pain was enough. It wasn't until years later that I began to comprehend the healing power of the natural world and the healing power of ritual. I came to see how important it is to follow our instincts for they lead us to nourish the seeds of life though they have not yet taken form. My short time with the Huichol was an initiation that I came to understand only as I looked back on it.

A Candle for All of God's Children

When I returned from Mexico, Christmas was approaching, blasting from every television and radio commercial, glaring from every newspaper page. An endless assault, besieging me to have a joyous holiday season. What a cruel joke.

Ivan, Elana's stepmother, Trudi, and I went to a meeting of the local chapter of Compassionate Friends. It turned out to be a candle lighting ceremony for the Christmas holidays. I will never forget the impact of walking into a room and seeing one hundred other bereaved parents. Never in my life have I experienced anything so potent. One hundred people, each holding a candle for the child they loved. How could anyone feel isolated and singled out by fate in the presence of so many who had lost so much?

A large Christmas tree stood in the corner with colorful Origami cranes gracing its branches. Each crane had the name of a child who had died written on its wing. It was quite a sight—delicate folded paper birds symbolizing peace and the eternal in Japan—in bright magenta, turquoise, yellow, and crimson encasing a perfectly contoured Douglas fir from Oregon's forests. I wondered how many other Christmas trees in remembrance of children who died stood in Compassionate Friends' meeting rooms across the country. I wondered how many other unnamed children didn't have an origami crane hanging on a tree in their memory. I looked to see if I could find Elana's name. Her godmother, Kris Olson, had made a donation in her memory and there was a little rainbow colored crane with "Elana" written on it. It still hangs on the dashboard of my car.

When it was time for the ceremony to begin, a lighted candle was passed around the circle as each person solemnly spoke the name of their child. Sad, drawn, courageous faces. Death doesn't discriminate. There were wealthy people from the West Hills, minorities from the inner city. There were people who gave the names of more than one child. I just looked at them. How could that happen to anyone, what kind of world is this where the fates are so brutal? I couldn't imagine how they had survived. It gave me new courage. But when the candle came to me, I froze. I couldn't say Elana's name. This is all a bad dream. I'm not standing here having to admit my daughter to this roll call from the heavens. Please, someone, make this not be true. Closing my eyes, summoning all my emotional strength, the force of sheer will power pushing the words out of my mouth, "Elana Gold, age sixteen, plane crash." I turned and lit the candle of the person next to me. When all the candles were lit, symbolizing how we light the way for each other, we stood in silent prayer.

In this community, in the presence of the immensity of others' grief, I could see for the first time that death is part of life even for the young. I realized that I am part of higher laws and larger events which govern our lives and over which we have little control. The burden became lighter because it is a burden we all share.

At other times, I'd watch bereaved parents on the evening news receive the support of the whole community because their child's death was the result of a tragic accident or a ruthless crime. I would become angry when the media turned it into a public mourning day in and day out. I knew I had no right to feel that way, but I did. Every child who dies deserves a community vigil, not just the child whose death reflects the violence in our midst. The child who dies after a long heroic struggle with cancer, or as Elana did, from a freak accident, is no less deserving of public protest, of community support. Every child who dies is ultimately a victim of chance.

As a culture we leave bereaved parents isolated. What I heard the most afterwards from well- meaning friends and acquaintances alike was "I didn't know what to say, I didn't know what to do." And we don't. I again found myself looking to the ancients in search of meaningful customs.

Waiting out the Holidays

I didn't do any of the traditional activities we had done as a family. I couldn't even light the Chanukah candles because Elana and I had lit them together from the time she was a toddler. All I could think about was how it felt to stand next to her, steadying her hand as she lit the Menorah. I wanted to be in a place where there was no Christmas, no Chanukah, a place where I wasn't bombarded by images of families coming joyfully together. The holiday season is an exponential magnification of the loss for the bereaved.

I managed to get through the month of December, but the rest of my life loomed before me with a resounding emptiness. There was nothing that drew me in anymore, nothing to keep me going. I was alone. I had no other children. *Was this my destiny?*. What have I done wrong? I felt condemned by fate, first as an only child myself, then as an "orphan" after the inevitable death of my parents, now childless. It was hard for me to tell Richard that his loving presence wasn't enough to give me a reason to go on living. His warm arms were soothing and the loneliness would have been unbearable without him, but the magnitude of Elana's loss was overriding. I was simply no longer tethered to life. At the same time, there was a restlessness, an urgency inside that said I needed to keep moving toward something or the emptiness would destroy me.

Quite by accident, I learned that a course in Shamanic healing that I had been interested in was being given at Esalen close to Elana's birthday in March. This was a two-week intensive program sponsored by the Foundation for Shamanic Studies and taught by a former academic anthropologist whom I had previously heard speak. I was struck by the irony of enrolling in a course that I wouldn't have had the time for until after Elana graduated from high school. Now here I was in what would have been the middle of her junior year with all the time in the world. I felt uncomfortable that I was gaining something by Elana's absence, prematurely taking advantage of the parental freedom that comes as a rite of passage when a child leaves home. On the other hand, the symbolism of traveling an unknown universe in search of healing on Elana's birthday was part of the new links I was trying to establish to give my life a meaningful structure.

All this agonizing was for naught because when I called to register the program was full and I was put on a waiting list. I was intensely disappointed. Only then did I realize how deeply I was being drawn to the study of shamanism and healing. I turned it over to the universe. If this was meant to be, I would get into the seminar. Nothing happened. Five days before the course was to begin, I received a call that a space had opened. I cleared my schedule, packed my things, and got on a plane.

Returning to Esalen

I arrived at Esalen full of anticipation. Esalen is in a spectacular setting, sitting high on the bluffs overlooking the Pacific on the Big Sur coastline. I had last been there ten years ago. There was a magic even then, although the place was well past the Sixties' heyday when it was at the center of the human potential movement. I retraced familiar steps across the huge expanse of lawn to the edge of the bluff. Despite my pain, or maybe because of it, as I stood in the shadow of the giant redwoods, looking out over the craggy cliffs at the vastness of the Pacific and its endless shoreline of riffled white lines, I felt immense gratitude for being surrounded by this magnificence. There is a power in this land, a magic to this place that evokes a sense of harmony with the universe. The beauty of nature comes into your bones here. A feeling of well being and vibrancy washed over me that I didn't think I was *ever* capable of experiencing again.

As I stood on the cliff, I thought about the last time I was at Esalen in 1982. I roomed with my friend Barbara whom I had met at a meeting of family therapists. She was the only person I knew at the time who had lost a child. I'll never forget sitting on her bed until the wee hours of the morning as she told me about her eight year-old daughter who had contracted bacterial meningitis and went from a healthy child to an oxygen tent in twenty four-hours, and died the next day. At the time I was young and frightened of death. I didn't think a person could survive losing a child. I knew I would surely die if anything ever happened to Elana, who was only five years-old at the time. That a healthy child could become ill and die in a day leaving a parent so utterly helpless and defenseless shook whatever false security held my world together. It took all my fortitude not to flee Barbara's presence.

Barbara's was a story of bravery, love, compassion and healing. She told me about the marigolds her daughter had planted for her that came into bloom on Mother's Day and remained in bloom for an extraordinary length of time. Marigolds became a symbol of her daughter and when she went to India and was greeted with leis of marigolds, she felt the flowers were leading her to a path. When she returned home, it became clear that she would adopt a child. She knew that she would die if she closed herself down to love and as painful as it was, the path to healing was the path of continuing to love, of opening her heart to the universe, not closing it down. Barbara's adopted daughter was nine- years old when I met her in 1982 and she had been singing and playing the guitar at spiritual and peace gatherings, receiving great joy from this. She described how through prayer and a love of God she had become whole, and how she had deep gratitude for every day of her life and the small joys and pleasures it brings.

Barbara was like a spirit being. There was a purity of soul, compassion and love that emanated from her that was beyond my grasp, foreign to anything I had ever experienced. I felt like I was being mentored, shown things about love and the larger purposes of life that I didn't understand. I was an innocent thirty-five year-old just out of a divorce, still struggling with my mother and grappling with men and relationships. Barbara had wisdom and a deep understanding of things that were only abstractions to me.

As I sat with Barbara the night she told me about her daughter's death, I had a terrifying thought. What if the cosmos had allowed us to find each other because she was to show me how it is possible to survive the death of a child? What if I was being prepared for something? The thought palpably spooked me. I tried to convince myself I was overreacting. Despite my rational efforts to dismantle this anxiety, I couldn't entirely shake it. It remained in the back of my mind and I breathed a sigh of relief when Elana passed her eighth birthday, the age at which Barbara's daughter had died.

And when at sixteen, Elana was killed in an instant, my thoughts turned to Barbara. My world ended that day. I wouldn't have known there could be another world had it not been for my friendship with Barbara. Her life had shown me it was possible to go on, that it was possible to bear such pain, and even heal from it. Knowing Barbara gave me the courage to face the emptiness and devastation of my life. I think about her often now.

Heartbeat, Drum Beat

I walked back to the main lodge for supper. The Esalen dining room with its rustic split log tables and beamed ceiling was a buzz. As I stood in the buffet line, I saw an acquaintance from my active days in alternative dispute resolution. What a shock to see a woman who worked for the American Bar Association here at Esalen carrying a drum and a rattle. We sat together at dinner and she told me that she also had lost a child. Her son died from a progressive disease at the age of twenty-six. We shared our stories, the laughter and bustle of the dining room completely shut out. That the very first person I encountered at Esalen had also lost a child was a coincidence I couldn't ignore. It was a wake-up call telling me to take notice, important things were going to happen here.

Excitement was in the air as people gathered in the morning for our first meeting. We sat in a circle, our drums and rattles by our side. I had never used my drum before. It was painted with an ancient petroglyph of three woman dancing and hung on my wall as art. Little did I know it was to become as sacred to me as a Stradivarius.

A candle was lit and the drumming began, slowly, evenly, in unison. Our eyes closed as we yielded to this ancient rhythm and allowed a song to arise from within. Soon there was only the steady beat of the drum, carrying us further and further away from ordinary reality. The resonant timbre of my own drum reverberated in my ear as I listened and waited for what needed to emerge from the inner depths to come forward as sound. After a few minutes, in a low soulful voice, I heard myself singing, "Whey ya whey ya, hey, hey hey; whey ya whey ya, hey hey; Whey ya whey ya, hey hey, hey; whey ya whey ya, hey hey." Over and over I sang this chant. My voice was strong and I felt a remarkable sensation of power. I had never sung like this. I can barely carry a tune. This song was coming from somewhere else.

There we were, forty-five people drumming and singing our own private struggle, our own private pain, our own private joy. Together and alone, an immense sounding, the drum a vehicle for crying, calling, praying. I felt my psyche was being entrained by an elemental force at once mysterious and familiar. The power of this drumming was primal. It transported me outside of time, outside myself, outside my pain. I felt strong, I felt healed. I have no other words for it. The drum calls the depths of the human psyche and spirit like no other sound. It carries our intention to the gods, to the innermost sanctum of our being. Sitting in this circle, I knew I had to know more about this ancient sounding. Yet when we stopped drumming and ordinary reality entered in, I looked around the circle at the faded jeans, tee shirts espousing environmental causes, expectant middle class faces, and thought maybe we were we just a bunch of Indian "wannabes."

Journey to the Spirit World

We lay down on the rug and covered our eyes with bandannas. The lights were turned out. Our teachers stood in the center and began drumming. We were journeying with our mind's eye into the spirit world to ask for guidance. This was the core practice of Shamanism. The steady beat of the drum carried us deep into trance, allowing us to leave ordinary reality and invoke a world beyond. On this journey, we were asking to be shown the destiny of souls. I took a deep breath and fixed the pillow under my head to get comfortable. We had done many journeys that week, retrieving lost souls, asking about the hidden power of plants or how to help heal an illness or physical problem. But this time we were asking to be shown what happens after death and I felt a little apprehensive.

I adjusted my position one more time and let the drum lead me to the quiet place inside, dropping me deeper and deeper into trance. I imagined myself at the moment after death as instructed and saw myself traveling up through the heavens out into the cosmos. It was very peaceful, not frightening as I thought it would be. I had a sense of being outside the boundaries of my body, of being pure consciousness. There was a feeling of enormous harmony and love. Higher and higher I went, floating gently until I broke through a white luminous matter.

All of a sudden, there was Elana, along with my parents, grandparents, and my Hungarian sheep dog, Pasjda. I greeted my parents and hugged them and ran towards Elana. We embraced and held each other for a long time, crying how much we missed each other. Sobbing, I told her how sorry I was, how I wanted it to be me, how I wanted to change places with her, that I would give up everything if she could return. I stepped back and looked at her. She appeared her age, but there was a tranquility and luminescence about her. She moved in slow motion and when she spoke her voice had the quiet authority of wisdom. She told me that she feels sad for me, but she is peaceful and in a good place and that I shouldn't worry about her. I asked her what happens here. She didn't answer. We held each other in a joyous embrace for what seemed like a very long time, then strolled arm in arm as I tenderly brushed the hair from her face. I didn't want to go, but the rapid beat of the drum summoned our return. I said goodbye to Elana and thanked my spirit guides. They told me to remember that the soul is eternal, that people live on in the hearts and minds of those who love them and in the good deeds they have left behind. I retraced my steps back to my starting point and returned to this world. When the drumming ended, I lay without moving. I didn't understand whether any part of what I saw on my visionary journey was "real," but I felt I had experienced a reunion with my daughter. On an emotional level, it was certainly real.

Ancient Healing

I had not begun this quest from a position of faith in a higher being or an afterlife. Prayer had not been part of my life. Shamanism appealed to me because it was not a religion, but one of the oldest practices of accessing the visionary mind to seek spiritual guidance and healing. Shamanic ability is based on cultivating trance states that access that often described unused 90 percent of our brain and on learning to trust spiritual forces one can never fully understand or know. As a rationalist and atheist, I was starting from ground zero. And what we did next was going to put reason to a test.

AH WEY, AH WEY, WEY, WEY, WEY. The chanting and drumming began. The "patients" were sprawled on the floor as we shook our rattles over them and called the spirits. We were learning shamanic extraction, a method used by indigenous healers to remove the spiritual causes of illness. Closing our eyes, we were to imagine the body as a tunnel and move our hands over it trying to sense areas that were dark, hot, or in which odd shapes and forms appeared, sometimes in the form of spiders or insects. We were to remove these "intrusions" which in shamanic terms were the causes of illness occurring when there was a spiritual vacuum, much as modern disease occurs in a weakened immune system.

I closed my eyes, envisioning my partner's body as a tunnel as we were instructed, and began vibrating my hand about six inches above the length of her body. Softly chanting to deepen my trance, I slowly moved my hand down the left side of her body and up the right side. At first I didn't see or feel anything. Uneasy, I thought, what if I can't do this? What if I don't see anything? As I became more focused and shut down my mental conversations, and remembered to let "spirit" guide me, I saw inclusions and dark spots in her pelvic region and right knee. They had no specific form, but appeared as amorphous dark images. I scanned her body again but didn't see or feel anything else. The drumming became faster signaling we should begin "extracting" the intrusions. Cupping my hands, I gathered up the energy field around the problem areas and cast it aside. I did this repeatedly, "removing" the intrusions until all the dark areas appeared clear.

It was hard for me to believe extracting these images was going to help anyone. Afterward, I learned my partner did have painful issues around pregnancy and also had problems with her right knee from an old injury. I was astounded by the accuracy of the "diagnosis," but expressed my doubts about whether there was any lasting benefit on a physical level from what we did. I was told that one can't predict how a spiritual healing will manifest on a physical level or in a person's life.

While I was quite skeptical about any hands-on healing, I was willing to concede that this ceremony with the intense drumming and chanting in the background, the candles and prayer, the loving intention, the gentle rattling and singing for the person's spirit, the calling in of sacred sources all seemed to have a positive emotional impact, even if it was only the power of suggestion. As it later turned out, the extraction conducted for me was a center point in my own healing.

When it was time to reverse roles, I lay down on the floor and closed my eyes. The chorus of drumming and chanting began as my partner started to shake her rattle over my body. I wondered what she would find. Would my body be riddled with intrusions because of my grief? Was disease incubating because of my vulnerability? How real was all this anyway? I decided to put my skepticism aside and welcome the opportunity to spiritually clear whatever blocks might be there. I relaxed and let myself surrender to the experience. I could sense her hands moving above me. I felt extraordinarily peaceful as she softly sang and rattled over my body. No one had ever attended to me like this before. When the extraction was over, she told me she saw a pervading blackness with menacing images appearing after a garden path had abruptly ended, but that a powerful white torpedo was aimed at them determined to destroy the blackness. Chills went down my spine. My life indeed felt like a garden path that had abruptly ended with the sudden death of my daughter and I did sense that I had a force field in the form of a determination to heal, a determination to push through the terrible darkness. The image of the white torpedo was extremely life affirming for me because until then I wasn't aware of the strength of my determination, or that it could see me through. I was barely conscious of it as a force in my life. I was concerned that my body would fail from grief, that I would succumb to serious illness like so many people I knew who had suffered profound loss. That she saw this "determination" in my body without knowing me at all as a person, engendered a fundamental trust in myself that I was going to survive, that I was not going to be ultimately undone by the darkness of my loss.

"Time Does Not Separate Us Now"

One afternoon two friends and I hiked through a canyon on the Big Sur coast. We came to a magnificent redwood that had been badly charred by lightening. It was a tree that stops you in your tracks, massive and imposing, the trunk perhaps four feet in diameter, its limbs miraculously penetrating the forest canopy. As we stood spellbound by this extraordinary tree, a white butterfly appeared. I looked at the butterfly and a certainty came over me that made the hair on my arms tingle. I told the others about the white butterfly at Elana's funeral and how its appearance had felt like a sign from Elana. Spiritual pilgrims that we were, we asked if the butterfly had a message for me. There was a profound stillness in the air as if all the forest's creatures held their breath. The butterfly circled near us and the message was "I am always with you. Time does not separate us now."

The appearance of the white butterfly did not feel like a mere coincidence. Esalen is a nesting place for the monarch butterfly and in the ten days that I had been there, I had not seen a single white butterfly. On our return, as we passed the same tree, three white butterflies suddenly flew across our path. What a gift. It was like Elana saying, "See I am not alone, I have friends." That was so much like her.

I felt joyful for this sign, but my grief was still too fierce for the full meaning to fill my heart. It wasn't until years later that I understood its truth. *She is always with me. Time does not separate us now.*

As the week progressed and we delved deeper into these ancient healing practices, it became apparent that one had to suspend judgement. I had to surrender more to the experience without forever questioning and analyzing what had occurred. Never one to take anything on faith, I could not accept that our shamanic visions were more than the projections of our own minds. I had yet to be convinced of the existence of "spirits."

The last day we did an ancient ceremony in the round house called the "healing drum." As we sat in the circle with candles and sage burning in the center, a drum was empowered through prayer to bring healing to the people who needed it. Anticipation hung in the air as two participants were selected to carry the drum around the circle, eyes closed, guided by the drum which was held out in front of them. The moment we began, the drum carriers raced all the way across the room as if they were being pulled. They stopped abruptly in front of me and began pounding the drum, beating and pounding in utter existential protest. The woman drum carrier began wailing unlike anything I have ever heard. This wail was so old, so deep, so penetrating, I knew I wasn't capable of allowing myself to sound it. Yet it was the wail that was inside me. It was the wail of all mothers who have lost their babies, and it came through this woman for all of us.

As I sat there sobbing, profoundly affected, a voice said, "We will always be with you, you can work with healing, you can be a shaman." The message was penetrating, clear, and felt like it came from outside myself. Stunned, I didn't know what to make of this. Was I hallucinating? I would never aspire to call myself a shaman, but I wanted to help people heal. I felt that I was being told that spirit had come to work with me and would remain with me. When I asked Michael Harner, the director of the program, about the voice that came in this ceremony, he said

105

you have to trust your experience. Trust, I thought. How can you trust something you don't understand? It took me a long time to realize that is just the point. You have to be willing to trust experiences that are outside your rational ability to fully comprehend them. He said that in spiritual work, you must be willing to live with the principle of ambiguity. You can never know for certain. That was not what I wanted to hear.

This healing drum ceremony marked for me the tentative beginning of my relationship with what is regarded as spirit, and those two weeks at Esalen marked the beginning of a commitment to spiritual development and a study of healing. I didn't know where this would take me, how it would evolve. I just knew that I was deeply drawn to this path and that Shamanism was the vehicle that could bring me closer to a relationship with cosmic presence and its power to heal, and most importantly to my daughter. I returned home with a sense of hope. I began to see there might be a way to put my broken life back together.

She Would Have Been Seventeen Today

March 1, Elana's birthday, a mild sunny day like so many other March firsts when February's chill gave way to the first scent of spring and her little playmates ran around the backyard eating ice cream and chasing bubbles.

She would have been seventeen. Friends gathered at the house. We planted a Weeping Cedars of Lebanon near the back door where I could see it from the desk in my den. Kate, looking tentative and fragile, wearing brown baggy pants and a tan sweater, read a poem she had written. Erika, Liz and Chessy, in charge of the music, blasted one of Elana's favorite songs, the Grateful Dead, *If I Had The World to Give* while we stood outside in a circle under the big maple tree listening to the words. The sun warmed our backs. Small pink buds poked through the leathery leaves on the camellia bushes and the fragrance of the andromeda wafted through the yard. Everyone was still grieving, still in shock. When the song was over, people milled about. I felt awkward. What is one supposed to do at a memorial birthday for a seventeen year-old? I didn't want this day to go unacknowledged. Her friends and the people close to us needed to do something. We were trying to celebrate Elana's life. That is what she would have wanted.

It was an odd mix of people. Close friends of her father's as well as mine, the strange legacy of divorce. This was the first time many of the people there were meeting Judy or Kate. I could feel their eyes on me when Judy and I embraced so warmly. I'm sure they wondered how I could feel so caring toward her when her husband was the pilot. My response is always, how can I not?

It was good to see Kate up and out. Despite her fragility, she was making remarkable progress. Five months after being in a coma, she was now in outpatient rehab and sitting in on a few classes at her old school. She had a limp and walked with a cane, but she was beginning to look like her old self. Her hair was growing back and was stylishly cropped close to her face. There was a small, barely visible scar on her chin. Pretty and freckled, the same sweetness was there. That was on the outside. She had to relearn everything from simple math to tying her shoes. She was lost. Many things in her past were gone forever. I had my arm around her as I introduced her, wondering if she would ever remember eighth grade graduation or the day she got her driver's license.

Lynn Osborne, the co-pilot's widow, came with Judy and Kate. She looked thin and pale and vulnerable. She was having a very hard time. Her high school sweetheart and all her dreams were gone and she could see nothing in her life. She wasn't able to work, she wasn't in school, she wasn't eating well, she was still afraid to be alone at night. For now, she was helping to care for Kate, driving her to appointments and physical therapy. She frequently stayed with Judy and Kate who were rambling around in a big old colonial house. I think they were her lifeline.

It was a hard day. Friends brought their families and young children ran around the back yard chasing balls. Conversation was awkward. People asked how was I doing. It took enormous energy to really answer the question. Sometimes I thought, do you really want to know, or do you want to me to protect you? Often I just said, "It's a little easier. I don't cry as much."

The fact of the matter was, I did cry as much.

Staying Away

Being home, I was thrown back into the familiar where missing Elana was again the foreground of my life. I wanted to be away from it all. I wanted to stay away from graduation ceremonies, from seeing Elana's friends grow up and go to college, from the toddlers with their coddling mothers in the pool at the athletic center, from Richard's son who was Elana's age and doing all the things she should be doing, from standing behind mothers and daughters, laughing and holding hands on the escalator at Nordstom's on a Saturday afternoon shopping excursion, from strangers who might ask me if I have any children. I wanted to stay away from soccer fields, from weddings, from new grandmothers. I wanted to stay away from the future I couldn't have. I wanted to stay away from the future Elana couldn't have. But where should I go?

I went to the trees. I felt peace in the embrace of the land. It was becoming my closest ally. When I sat cross legged against the gnarly four foot girth of one of the ancient ones, I felt the profound connection to the earth. I was drawn to a sense of the eternal. Linear time locked in my pain. The experience of timelessness freed me from it. Here in the wilderness, there were no memories of the past or thoughts of the future. I'd dig my fingers into the damp earth and endlessly watch a colony of ants bearing heavy loads, threading their way along huge logs in their march toward home. In the silence of the forest, the laws of nature penetrated my very being. The giant redwoods spoke to me. They told me that all life is a cycle. Death and rebirth, darkness and light. They told me that spring will come, it always does. As I walked in the old growth forest looking at towering limbs splintered down the middle, black and charred by lightening, still reaching ever majestically toward the heavens, I'd lift my head one more time. Nature had become my teacher.

Compatriots

One day Judy invited me, Lynn Osborne, and her sister to go for a walk in the Japanese Garden while Kate was at an appointment. It was a grey drizzly day as we strolled along narrow stone paths meandering through bamboo waterfalls, ponds of lily pads, and lushly sculpted weeping pines. We rested on a small bench in front of a miniature Japanese pagoda. It was one of the few times we talked easily about the accident. It was always easy to talk about Kate, but hard to talk about the plane crash itself. There were still unanswered questions about the cause of the accident and undoubtedly unresolved feelings about responsibility. I really don't know how Judy felt. It was something we couldn't talk about. But Lynn talked a lot that day. She had actually been back to the airport several times querying pilots and other personnel about what they saw. She had looked at the runway, studied the terrain, and even examined the wreckage in the farmer's field. She had no real answers. The plane crashed within thirty seconds of take-off. All anyone heard was the motor suddenly cut off. The plane was already out of sight.

For me to have gone anywhere near the airport or to have viewed the wreckage would have been like falling into a black hole. It was five years before I went near the place that robbed my daughter of her life. But the steering controls had been found broken off in her husband's hand, and Lynn, who had a fair amount of experience flying with him, was driven to understand what went wrong, who was at the controls and why they couldn't take the plane out of the nose dive. It troubled us all that the plane crashed under such seemingly benign conditions.

I could see that Lynn and I were both still playing out the "what ifs." Sitting on the bench, words she needed to say were finally uttered, "If you hadn't allowed Elana to fly, I would have been the one in her seat. Now I'm still here and Elana isn't."

"Lynn, you can't do this to yourself, this is the way it was. You have every right to be alive."

"But even if I had gone along for the ride, the plane would have been lighter because I wouldn't have had any luggage. It might have made it."

I put my arm around her and held her tight, saying, "We'll never know."

For me the burning questions were why couldn't the accident have been survivable. The plane had barely gained altitude. I questioned Lynn as if she were an authority because she was the only one who had gone back to the crash sight.

"How high was the plane in relation to those trees over there when it lost power? Were the seat belts ripped out? How do you think Kate was positioned that she survived? Had Keith flown into that airport before, did the people there consider Sisters a difficult airport, had there been other accidents there? If only small planes were required to be equipped with shoulder harnesses instead of seatbelts, I bet they would have survived."

Of course Lynn didn't have the answers to my questions. All that everyone could say was that this was a crash that shouldn't have happened.

Judy talked about how Stu went over the altitude density calculations many times before he left, inquiring

110

about Elana's weight, the weight of the girls' book bags and luggage. Lynn said Keith knew how to handle the altitude conditions and that many small airports had difficult configurations. Both Keith and Stu had talked about the terrain and knew they had to bank to the left immediately at the end of the runway, but Keith wasn't as familiar with an amphibian plane, and neither knew the airport well, and maybe when they got into trouble they didn't react fast enough, or maybe there was nothing they could have done. With her pale blue eyes brimming, Lynn told us how she and Keith had made an agreement the night before he died that this would be the last flight he would take over the mountain in a single engine plane because it made her nervous.

It was a helpful visit for me. The four of us walked in the drizzle that afternoon in teary silence, sometimes talking, laughing, or stopping to smell a flower. We looked like other visitors, but we were in slow motion. We could have been characters in a Fellini movie—*three women, thrown together by destiny, a dark untold past reflected in their gaze; the fates cast them cards from the same hand; how were they each going to play them?*

Did I Do Enough?

One rainy afternoon I was sitting at the computer in my den remembering how I used to lean back in my chair looking out the window, captivated by watching Elana kick a soccer ball around in the back yard. She ran circles around herself with the intensity and innocence of times gone by. It was a memory I cherished, even then. I remember thinking there is not much time left, she's in her junior year of high school, these unselfconscious childhood moments running through the grass in the sunshine were almost over. I wanted this scene, the simple childish delight as she practiced soccer by herself, to be indelible in my mind. Now I thought, why didn't I get up and play with her more? We had a good time when I did. Little did I know I wouldn't have any more chances.

A deep sigh. I didn't do enough, my work got in the way. I wish I had gone to more of her soccer games, track meets, ski races. I wish I had been more involved in her school, I wish I could have been home after school when she was little. I should have baked more brownies. I should have read to her more. I should have taken her to the Enchanted Forest. The list can be endless.

Stop torturing yourself, you can make yourself crazy. She was an only child. Look at what you gave her. You took her to plays, to concerts, to the beach—to Florida, New York, Disneyland. She even went to Le Louvre. She saw the Eiffel Tower. You gave her opportunities, ballet, gymnastics, the piano, the flute, art classes, tennis, skiing, a good education. You taught her to sew, cook, and think for herself. You loved her dearly and she knew it. No one is a perfect parent. No one ever feels they did enough. No parent can look back without any regrets.

This scenario replayed itself each time I drifted from my work and gazed out the window at the empty yard. I flashed back on all the times she was out there playing and where was I? All the times I couldn't pick her up after school or wouldn't take her downtown. Finally after weeks of this, I made peace. I forgave myself for the more I could have been, for the more I could have done. I know I was a very good mother, not perfect, but I was there for her. She was the most important thing in my life. My mistake was that I thought I would have her forever.

In Memoriam

I knew I had to do something that would keep Elana's memory alive, but I didn't know what. I also knew I had to find a way to remain connected to Elana's world, but I didn't know how. To never see the other parents, the soccer coach, the teachers in the school that had been like a family for eleven years, to have the connective links to a community of wonderful people whom my child brought into my life so abruptly severed would have been horrible. A child so young hardly leaves her mark, and I was afraid that Elana could just disappear.

Her friends had planted a memorial tree in the lawn of Lincoln High School where she had just transferred as a junior, and a lovely wooden bench with a memorial plaque had been placed in the courtyard of Catlin Gabel School where Elana had been since preschool. As deeply appreciative as I was of these loving gestures by her friends, I needed to feel Elana's death would somehow contribute to the living. I decided to create a student environmental restoration project in her name. Elana had deep concerns about the environment and this was a way for her to be remembered and for others to benefit. A memorial program was established through Catlin Gabel School in conjunction with the U.S. Forest Service. Our focus was going to be the restoration of a degraded area in the Rock Creek Basin on the east side of Mount Hood and the program would take a group of twenty-five students for one week each summer to work on the site.

I drove up to the mountain that first June, sleeping bag in tow, with great anticipation. I was doing something that would make a difference. I felt in my heart that this would heal me. For six days we cut back thick underbrush along fencing for controlling cattle, drove spikes in the ground to repair wire fencing protecting the riparian zone, and dragged fallen logs down to the stream bank to create chuck dams for fish habitat. The ticks were out and the sun was brutal, but the work felt good and the students accomplished an amazing amount.

I felt extremely pleased about the program and grateful for the efforts of the coordinators Dave Corkran and Wendy May, two of Elana's favorite teachers. We received tremendous support from the Barlow ranger district with fish biologists, botanists, and rangers working with us

113

every day. But the magical benefits I expected for myself, that somehow my pain would be lifted as the first restoration project was completed, did not occur. I went home after a week of clearing, grading, fencing and replanting a stream habitat that had been destroyed by cattle, and wept.

I don't know why I thought realization of this project would be a turning point in my grief, the key to healing I so desperately sought, but I did. Even the last night when we sat under the stars and talked about Elana and about death, as powerful and moving as this exchange was (the high point as many of the students later reported), there was no great sigh, no revelatory insight that reshaped the interior of this loss.

I realize now that there is no one thing that heals, there is no one thing that makes a difference. It is all the little things you do, and do them you must. Not to have taken a memorial action would have been worse. I needed to mark the event in a way that honored my child and created something out of death that is of value. The healing is knowing that I've done this—my last act as a mother going the distance for her child.

Heart Medicine—the Healing Power of Music

There were days when I was working around the house that I played the same CD all afternoon. It was as if I was sounding my body back to wholeness. It could be Mozart's "Requiem," or the 17th century viola music written by Saint Colombe after the death of his young wife, or Michael Nyman's "The Piano," the mysterious lament of a woman locked inside her own world. It was far more profound than being in the mood for sad music. It was a driving force instinctively drawing me toward another broken soul. Whatever anguish the composer mastered was what I needed to master, and if I listened long enough, perhaps I, too, could be released from its grip. These pieces of music seized upon the immobilizing sadness and dislodged it from my cells. They met me in the place of no words. They had the power to transform my sorrow into a thing of beauty, moving it out of self-pity into something more noble. This music was heart medicine. It was a prescription no doctor could fill.

I frequently listened to Eric Clapton's song, "Tears in Heaven," written after his four year-old son fell to his death from an upper story apartment building window. I wanted to know how he resolved the pain, how did he go on? I'd stop what I was doing to listen to the words whenever it played on the radio. When I bought the CD, I even put my ear next to the speaker listening for something I might have missed. Surely he had an answer. But there was only his sad song and the hope that there would be no more tears in heaven. I guess that was his answer.

One Saturday I was sprawled out on the living room floor working on an art project listening to the soulful Cajun music from the soundtrack of the movie, "Passion Fish"—a beautiful John Sayles film about a young actress paralyzed by an automobile accident. The story was about her return home to the bayou to spew her rage and lick her wounds. The music magnetized me. Over and over I hit the replay button. I listened to it the entire day, and for weeks afterward. It was like a great thirst. The music mirrored the path from utter desolation to coming to terms with tragedy. I think my psyche was trying to decode it and unconsciously drive its soulful message of hope into my bones. Then as intensely as I played this and other music I would abandon it, as if something was healed and I no longer needed its emotional resonance.

Our bodies and psyches intuitively recognize music that is healing, that has the resonance, energy, or power we need. We are drawn to music that shows us that place inside where we need to be. We all need heart medicine. Whatever it is, it reaches deep into the soul and transforms the pain. Our sorrow becomes the sorrow of the ages and it is no longer ours alone to bear.

I was getting used to the house without Elana. What it was like to have her around was no longer in my bones. Time had fogged the visceral traces of her memory. I remember in the beginning saying to myself that it would be unthinkable to lose the feeling of her presence, the sound of an adolescent in action, laughing, swearing, looking for lost things. But you do. It happens so gradually, imperceptibly, you hardly notice it is gone. Perhaps that is what is meant by "time heals." It dulls the memory. Our loved one is no longer viscerally beside us and it doesn't hurt as much.

One afternoon in late June, after I had returned from the memorial project, Kate and Lynn Osborne, the co-pilot's widow, dropped by my house. They were absolute pictures of loveliness, wearing bright new summer outfits and oversized sunglasses, their blond heads bobbing under the seductive slant of new hats. It was a remarkable contrast to the dark days of the past winter. Kate was making progress and learning to drive again. Lynn had gotten back to the dance studio. It had been nine months in hell and it wasn't over yet. Lynn still frequently stayed at Kate's because she was afraid to be at home alone at night and Kate still had amnesia about various aspects of her life before the accident. But today the girls looked beautiful. It was the first joyful excursion since the accident, their first step outside their grief, and they radiated. They had been shopping and bought new hats, the soul's secret sign that it is coming back to life.

I wanted to remember how they looked. I shot a roll of film as they posed toying with their hats. Tubs of flowers were in the background and sun streamed though the trees highlighting their blond hair. Slightly tanned, each lightly freckled, their hands coyly draped over their knees, they turned this way and that with the utter abandon of youth. It was one of those times, a freeze frame, where the truth is hidden and there is only the moment. And a

116

remarkable moment it was, two young women on the threshold of life, delivered from death's watch. We never needed to say what this moment was about. We three always knew what was in each other's hearts.

The Unfillable

In August, a client was referred to me whose sixteen year-old daughter had been killed in a car accident about the same time Elana died. I deliberated a long time about whether I was ready to work with a client whose circumstances were so close to mine. When a very attractive woman about my age walked into my office, for the first time in years I felt anxious and unsure of myself as a therapist. How could I help her when my own pain still was so real, so unresolved? In our first meeting, she told me about the accident. Her daughter and three friends were returning from a day of skiing. A car crossed over the center line, out of control on the ice. Her daughter died immediately. She never got to see her. She talked about how depressed and lonely she felt, how she banters to hide it, and can't seem to pull herself together. Her friend persuaded her to get professional help.

I stared at her pretty face, at her dark eyes straining to keep the tears from spilling. Sitting back in my chair, a heavy sigh escaping, I thought, how am I going to help her? I can't take away her grief, just as no one could do that for me. She showed me her daughter's picture. Sparkling dark eyes, long auburn hair, and a smile like her mother's. The eyes and smile tell it all, another bright radiant one, just like Elana. Damn it, no one is immune. They are all so innocent and hopeful and extraordinary when death snatches them. I didn't try to hide the tears that welled in my eyes. She told me how her daughter who died was the one with whom she had a special bond, a special camaraderie. They loved the same things, had similar personalities and could talk about anything. Her surviving daughter, who would soon be graduating from high school, was more like her husband. They were interested in science and sports, things that she was not, leaving her feeling even more alone in the family. There was a huge hole in her life. She had no career or job, her life had centered on her girls. She faced an empty future. She saw absolutely no way to fill the void.

As I sat listening to her, I knew this was a void that couldn't be filled. Nothing can replace a child. But I also knew it had to be filled. It sounded trite to suggest thinking about the future, what she could draw gratification from, what might make her future meaningful when the immensity of her daughter's absence was everywhere. We looked at each other for a long time. Finally I said there comes a time when ultimately there is nothing else to do but to try to fill the unfillable. I think I must have been speaking to both of us.

I met with her once or twice after that. She went on vacation and then I didn't hear from her. I am not sure why she didn't continue. Perhaps she got what she needed, or perhaps not.

Drumming Alone

I continued my shamanic studies at home. I was drawn to the power of these rituals and spiritual practices. They eased my pain. They opened up a mysterious world that I wanted to enter and understand. What exists beyond our acculturated perceptions of reality and the limited use of our sensory apparatus? Are there intercessory intelligences out there? Can consciousness act outside the body? Is the mind capable of healing others? What is the soul, and is it eternal? And most importantly, where is Elana in this cosmic soup?

I read all I could about shamanism and healing, all the while allowing myself to be drawn into the mysteries of the spirit world. Often in my darkened living room I drummed alone at night journeying to the other realms. When the house was quiet, I would light a candle and burn sage, bending over the smoke, breathing in deeply all that can purify, my whole being welcoming the familiar infusion. An inner stillness would come almost instantly. Sitting on my knees, I would begin to beat a gentle rhythm on the drum, calling in the powers from beyond, praying and asking for guidance. *Please help me, I am so lost, please help me find what I am to do, a path of healing.* Drumming myself deeper into trance, traveling up through veils of white, carried to the stars by a mythical being, held in a cradle of love. A great warmth radiated through my being and I melted into the lightness of omnipresent love, floating into eternity in a great dream. I rested in this cosmic embrace until I didn't need to anymore and then floated back down to this world. They felt like healings, real or imagined. When I opened my eyes, my body felt more whole. When I put the drum down, the immovable weight of this grief had been shoved aside.

As a therapist, I could see the psychological benefits of shamanic practice. But it was not until I was in a sweat lodge with a Lakota medicine man that I became convinced of the existence of spirits and powers from other realms.

The Eagle Spirit

In September, a few days before the first anniversary of Elana's death, I went to the Sierras for a gathering with Wallace Black Elk, a well known Lakota medicine man. The spiritual grandson of Nicholas Black Elk, the great medicine man and visionary of the 1930's book, *Black Elk Speaks,* Wallace Black Elk was controversial amongst his own people for his willingness to share their religion, but respected as a powerful healer by those interested in native teachings and earth spirituality. I had recently read a new book about him and was glad to have an opportunity to meet him.

119

We prepared for a Sweat Lodge, an ancient purification ceremony in which you gather and pray in a small womblike structure, close to earth, in utter darkness, while hot rocks are sprinkled with water. The leader sings prayers and calls the powers of the cardinal directions in each of four rounds. The suffocating heat pushes you to the edge of your endurance; you feel like you are going to die. But this is part of the purification; somehow emptying yourself by facing and going past your limit.

With a backdrop of the jagged Sierras against a piercing blue sky and the invigoration of crisp mountain air at the 7,000 foot altitude, we prepared all day for the ceremony; building the lodge with bent willow and blankets, cooking the sacred food, gathering the wood for the fire and the stones which would heat the lodge. We made hundreds of prayer ties, made by placing small amounts of tobacco inside pieces of red and white cloth which were then tied to a long string. A prayer was sent with the tobacco as we folded it into each piece of cloth. The ties were hung in the lodge representing our prayers and offerings to the Great Spirit. Everything was done precisely as grandfather Black Elk instructed, precisely as the spirits instructed him.

When evening came, we filed into the sweat lodge through the tiny door and sat on the ground crowded against each other. The fire keeper carried in the hot rocks with a shovel and piled them in the center. The flaps were closed, water was sprinkled on the rocks, and the ceremony was begun. The prayers for healing of family and friends, and for those of us who had lost family, including Black Elk whose adult son had been killed earlier that summer, were very solemn. Black Elk sang in Lakota as we went around the circle offering our own prayers. As water continued to be sprinkled on the rocks, the heat became impenetrable. After a while it was all there was. As I sat crouched against other sweaty bodies, clothes soaked, singing and crying out in prayer, barely able to breathe, unable to move, not knowing how much longer I could hold on, trying desperately to make peace with the suffocating heat, I heard a flapping sound as if something was circling inside the lodge. Staring at the blackness I could see nothing. Just then, I felt a slight breeze and was fanned by what felt like a feather brushing my face. This was not my imagination. I knew there was a supernatural presence in the lodge. The sound of a bird's flapping wings continued for several minutes. The eagle spirit was present. It was astounding. I had never experienced physical evidence of "spirit,"or of the supernatural. As I continued staring into the darkness, there were flashing bluish white lights which had the appearance of fireflies. I had read that when a powerful shaman calls the spirits these flashes of light frequently appear. I was now fully alert, diverted from the discomfort of not being able to breathe or move.

The door of the lodge opened, we cooled off, and more hot rocks were brought in. No one said a word. The door closed and the singing and praying resumed. I heard the sound of rattling, but I knew there was no rattle or drum inside the lodge. Grandfather Black Elk continued to pray to the spirits and passed around the pipe, the most sacred part of the ceremony. Just then, the rattling moved directly in front of me and I could feel a magnetic field pulsating around my hands and knees as the rattling continued. I didn't move. I didn't know what this was, but felt spirit was somehow acknowledging me. Black Elk started talking about the messages the spirits gave him. It was hard to understand what he was saying, harder still to understand what he meant. His voice was muffled, as if he were in a trance. He said something about my daughter, that the Eagle was holding her safely against its breast and that she had a smile on her face. He kept saying she was safe and happy and how the Eagle was holding her and protecting her. I didn't understand what he meant by this. Was her spirit here, could I talk to her? I didn't dare ask. He said that she is watching me and wants me to be happy and is sad when I am sad.

Later when the ceremony ended and we were talking outside around the fire, everyone commented in utter amazement about hearing the sound of the eagle flapping its wings, being brushed with a wing and feeling the breeze as it went by. Everyone saw the lights flash and several people heard the rattling, but no one else felt the pulsating field in front of them. Black Elk said that many spirits came to that lodge because the people had suffered so much and the prayers were so deep. The spirits were letting us know they were there.

This experience was compelling. I had read about powerful medicine men and shamans and the astonishing things they could do, but I had never witnessed the supernatural. The presences in the sweat lodge shifted my beliefs about the existence of the supernatural, of the manifestation of divine mystery. It affirmed that the shamanic work with "spirit" was not just a function of our own mind. It strengthened my hope that Elana was out there somewhere, a part of it all, and that maybe I could communicate with her.

The Give-away

The power of unseen forces played its hand one more time in a ceremony called the "give-away" which we did the following morning before we left. The give-away teaches us to release our need to hold the things we own and to trust that we will receive what we need. Each person was to bring a gift to be given away. The gifts were to be passed around the circle while Wallace Black Elk drummed. The drum would stop three times, and on the third time, you were to keep the gift you held in your hand.

We were to select something that had importance to us, and in the interconnected web of the ceremony the gift would go to the right person. I choose a rose quartz crystal heart that had been given to me to help heal my heart. Wallace Black Elk's gift was a medicine bag crafted from a small gourd. It was made by his sister, who was also a medicine woman and was used to help children heal. We all sensed the power of this gift.

As the drumming began and the gifts were slowly passed around the circle, anticipation rose. We knew that what we were about to receive was to have special meaning because of the intention of the ceremony. The drum stopped the first time after the gifts had gone completely around the circle. You could sense that all eyes were on Grandfather's medicine bag. The drumming resumed for one more round and stopped. Again you could sense all eyes on the medicine bag. Black Elk closed his eyes and resumed drumming as the gifts were slowly passed from hand to hand for the last time. The medicine bag was moving closer to me. I fought my desire to receive it, respecting the importance of the unseen forces and chance, but I had an uncanny feeling it would go to one of two other women or to me. I didn't think I was ready to work with the power of such a gift and tried to release any desire I had to receive it. As the drumming intensified, I could see the medicine bag was clearly going to pass me. When it came into my hands I smiled and turned to give it to the next person. The drum stopped. I was holding it.

This did not feel like pure chance. The other two women came up to me and said they also had felt it would come to one of the three of us. We smiled knowingly at each other. This was the way Grandfather and the spirits wanted it to happen. The question was, what would this mean for me? How was I to use the gift? Did it mean that someday I would work with children? Was I being guided? I took this gift to be a sign to stay on my path. After all, this was not like graduate school where the course of study was predictable—three years, forty-five credits, clinical internship, dissertation, exams. One doesn't know what the future holds or how the path of knowledge will unfold. I had to trust in something I didn't understand, and I wasn't very good at that. Yet, this always seemed to be

123

the message. I was struggling for certainty, begging for guidance, and when signs occurred, I never really understood what they meant or what I was supposed to do.

Walking with a Foot in Death's Doorway

That first year, I co-existed in the world of life and the world of death. There were periods when life's activities took on a familiar rhythm. I became absorbed by the demands of work. I would begin to feel normal. Always I'd awaken as if from a dream to the reality of my loss. Other times, I needed to be close to the presence of death. I wanted to be near Elana. I wanted to allow myself time to mourn and be with my grief. I spent afternoons reading— metaphysics, books about healing, mystical religions and practices. I listened to sacred choral music. These were very satisfying afternoons. My tears were near at hand, soft and unencumbered, my sorrow soothed by surrendering to it.

And always I would need to respond to the demands of this world. New divorce clients calling in distress about conflict with their spouse over the custody of children, child support, or who was going to move out of the house. Requests to teach workshops or be on a panel. Movies, dinners, social commitments with friends. No matter what I was doing, death walked silently beside me. I felt like I was split in half: part of me held death's hand, part of me participated in life. Regardless of how absorbed I was, I knew my involvement in activity was only a temporary distraction from the deeper resonance of my life. I knew I could be summoned back in an instant because everything around me was a reminder of Elana. My grief always broke apart my everyday world.

I participated in daily life because I had to, but I was really on a quest in search of my daughter and in search of healing. Even though a year had gone by, I still burned with questions about her death. What did her last words

124

mean? Did she foresee her death, was it her time? Does her death have karmic meaning for me? I couldn't let it go. I would have no peace until I understood more, until I had unequivocal communication from her.

The chords between us now were the chords between the worlds. My life was taking a strange new course and I was being drawn into a discourse with death.

PART IV: Amended Realities
Year Two

The vine maples had turned a bright orange, the al-
ders were dropping their leaves, and the sun beamed down
on freshly mowed lawn. I held a large shovel in my hands
and plunged it into the ground opening a cavity in the
yard near the kitchen window. Richard and I tenderly lifted
a small Weeping Spruce and placed it in the ground. September 29, 1992, the first anniversary of Elana's death.
In Judaism, one year marks the end of mourning, the time
when the bereaved is permitted and encouraged to fully
renew a life without the deceased. But, I felt no more ready
to fully embrace life without Elana than to walk on hot
coals.

A few close friends gathered at the house for dinner.
I cooked Elana's favorite food, spaghetti, from scratch, the
way she liked it. No Mamma Leoni shortcuts in a jar, even
now. As I stood at the counter chopping vegetables, the
voice which shadows me echoed inside. *Why do you bother
with these rituals. Can't you see your spiritual pursuits
aren't working. You're still in pain. You have no answers.
You haven't accepted her death.*

I stirred the sauce, clenching the spoon, the anger
rising. For a whole year, I had desperately prayed for a
teacher, for guidance, a message from Elana, something
to show me the way out of the abyss, something that said
this is how you reconcile the loss of a child, this is how
you recover. Why had the universe not responded more?
Where were my answers? The shamanic work, though it
helped, tendered ambiguity. I sought certainty, something
that said, "This is what will heal your broken life."

After dinner, I sat outside by the small memorial tree
we had planted, its delicately draped and twisted branches

almost touching the ground as if in nature's own prayer. I fantasized about running away, traveling in Europe or Asia, drifting to a place where I could lose myself, sit and stare vacantly in a crowded café, on an isolated beach, or wander aimlessly through small hillside villages until I didn't need to anymore. A place where I didn't have to participate, where I could be the outsider whom I had become, where I could go deeper into being on the sidelines.

I imagined drifting into oblivion, floating as in a dream for months or years until I was ready to come back. But I knew I'd never pick up and leave. I knew I didn't have the courage to relinquish the security of the familiar to face endless nights alone in strange and unaccustomed quarters. I felt inauthentic. After all, I chastised, didn't enlightenment require sacrifice? If you want spiritual revelation maybe you need to separate yourself from the material world, live in the Amazon jungle for a year, the Australian outback, or a monastery in Tibet. I closed my eyes picturing the serenity of sitting in lotus position high atop a holy mountain or walking the primal forests of a Gauguin painting. Then I thought about the primitive conditions, scorching heat, disease carrying insects, wild animals, malaria, dysentery. The appeal and the apprehension were equal weights on a seesaw holding me in place. I was stuck, no answers and no guts.

I lay down on the grass curled up in a ball, weary. I dug my fingers into the dirt, watching an ant crawl on my wrist. Soft tears melted into the soil. *I give up, I just fucking give up.* I am lost. I have no place to go. I cannot will the pain away. I cannot command my destiny to be revealed.

I rolled over on my back, staring up into the immensity of the pale night sky. The ache, the driving, agonizing questions bled out of my body into the earth. Something let go and it suddenly became clear, as if the cosmos was speaking, when you are lost, what you want most is to be found, saved from the unknown. I was fighting being lost, expecting a revelation, a singular turning point, where peace and acceptance would enter my heart, where the answers I sought would be unmasked and lift my pain. In one of those near epiphanies where the obvious becomes apparent, I realized that the path toward healing was a journey not a destination. I saw that I had no choice but to surrender to where I was, lost, untethered, hovering above the familiarity of the life I knew.

A strange calm came over me. I exhaled the incessant demand to know where I was going and what I was going to do now that Elana was gone. I realized that a journey through darkness is just that. All you can do is keep on moving and looking for the light. The path reveals itself in small, unsuspecting ways.

It is the archetypal journey into the underworld and the perils are as great as any physical voyage into unknown and distant lands. It is a journey all bereaved parents make—in our own way, in our own time. Some make it on foot, others travel the interior route, many never leave home.

Healing Community

In one of those moments when the questions were still burning and the emptiness was big, the phone rang. A space had opened in a three-year training program in shamanic healing sponsored by the Foundation for Shamanic Studies, which had sponsored the course I took at Esalen. I had been on the waiting list for nine months.

It was a fine October day in 1992 shortly after the first anniversary of Elana's death when I joined the group. We met twice a year for a week at a ranch in Northern California. I knew many people from other Foundation seminars and it was nice to see familiar faces. The people in this program were very committed to shamanic practice and were taking risks to introduce this work in institutional settings. There were people who worked with hospice, with drug and alcohol programs, other psychologists and therapists, physicians, and nurses. There were artists, engineers, contractors, physicists, a videographer, and a woman who was the first licensed female plumber in the state of California. It was a group whose common thread was a commitment to spiritual growth and a desire to help others.

This program was an anchor. I knew every six months I would be returning to this little hacienda with its collection of Mexican masks and artifacts on the walls, taking my familiar place in the circle. Each time I was here I walked the land, back to the places where the ache in my heart had been softened by nature's gifts. I hiked the narrow wooded trail past the bay laurel down to the stream. I jogged through the meadow in the knee high grasses to the top of the ridge by the big oak tree. Even just having tea with friends in the little courtyard framed by adobe walls and an orange tile roof; being here had the restorative power of place. This *was* my healing community.

Here in the glorious sunshine looking out over the rolling hills and lush green pastures of California's prime wine country, in a community of like-minded people, I had moments of deep calm. In the afternoon I often sat alone up on the top of the ridge by the big oak tree. Nothing to distract me. I simply sat, the warm sun on my back, gazing out over the sweeping panorama of this verdant valley carved from volcanic peaks. A sense of bigness enveloped me. It overtook my senses. I imagined what it must have been like for the first people to come upon this glorious valley. I imagined what this land, now known as California, must have been like in the beginning of time. I thought...she is out there somewhere. In this silence, I could feel her. In this immensity, she didn't seem so far away. Here on this hillside, in this community, I found a way to relate to her spiritually. Here the white butterflies came to me. At home the full physical reality of her absence was ever-present.

My soul found a resting place here. There was a feeling of coming home, to a place where the distance between people closed, where you could reach into the inner stillness and feel the breath of angels. I took my professional identity off. The trees and rocks spoke to me here. It was hard to return to a time-ordered world which separated me from experiences of the infinite, which separated me from her.

I came home from the first meeting not knowing how I was going to incorporate this work into my life. This wounding was not just leading me to a study of healing, it was requiring it of me. I couldn't pick up the life I had. Grief had cracked me open. A deep intuition and compassion had been unlocked. I had developed an almost mystical relationship to nature. The sacredness of all creation, a mere abstraction when I was with the Huichol in Mexico a year ago, was now in my bones. I was no longer the same person I was before Elana died.

I don't think anybody around me really understood this. *Oh, it's good you are traveling, oh it's good that you have become interested in something like Shamanism. Of course you are never the same after losing a child.* They were well meaning and caring. But even with my oldest friends, I could see the doubt in their eyes when I spoke about my shamanic experiences or spiritual pursuits. They would never really say it, but at times I sensed they thought these were the desperate endeavors of a mother who couldn't accept the death of her child. Even though we had a long history together and loved each other, they still had young families. The focus of our lives and the core of who we were was becoming more and more divergent. There was a whole new level of my being that I couldn't share with those closest to me. I had to figure out how to live these two realities. I had to figure out how to incorporate who I was becoming with who I was.

Two Separate Worlds

I missed the shamanic community that gathered at

the ranch. Richard, though interested and supportive, was simply not on a spiritual path. He still had the stresses of work and his children to usher through high school. I wished we shared spiritual pursuits just as I am sure he wished I was the way I used to be. Richard is a land use attorney and consultant involved in public policy issues. He was active in areas that didn't matter to me anymore. While I, too, had to work and earn a living, I had dropped out of all committee work, writing, lecturing, and national projects. My attention had turned inward. Our paths in life seemed to be diverging and this produced a certain strain. Though it was difficult to talk about, we knew we needed to give ourselves more time before trying to evaluate our future together. I suppose that was an attitude I was beginning to adopt about other things as well.

I tried to figure out if there was a way to integrate what I had been studying with my work as a therapist. A few friends had became interested in what I was doing. I began to work shamanically in the house with people who came to me by word of mouth who had suffered an injury or trauma and were interested in a spiritual approach to healing. I kept this very separate from my downtown clinical practice and I did not accept money. It almost felt like a secret life.

One week in particular, two young women who had been in car accidents called. One of them, a friend's twenty-five year-old daughter whose car had rolled off an icy embankment asked if I could help. She was facing knee surgery and was frightened, but even more than that she didn't feel she had emotionally recovered from the trauma of the accident. Her mother said she hadn't been the same since it happened. One afternoon, my friend and her daughter came over to the house. I lit a candle and burned sage as she stretched out on a bed of pillows in the middle of the living room floor. As I sat gently singing and rattling for her, decidedly aware of the vibrancy of this young woman that had vanished, her youth reminding me of my own daughter, I closed my eyes and called out silently in prayer, *Elana, are you with me?*

A song moved through me, cradling her spirit, calling to her soul, calming her fears. It was not I who sang so beautifully, but something from beyond, born of pure intention and love. I felt blessed. The loving energy that came through me, for this sweet young woman, was healing us both.

Forged Bonds

I saw Judy Moore fairly frequently. The accident was a profound bond for me. Our destinies had been forever linked by that Lake 250 amphibian plane. I felt less alone with what had happened when I was around Kate and Judy. We'd have dinner from time to time, pooling our leftovers. The walking wounded, cooking and not tasting, spilling and burning, laughing at our new found incompetencies.

I'd usually stop by their house, lettuce in hand. My house felt empty when Richard wasn't there. Judy's kitchen had the inviting warmth and informality that makes you want to stay. She had made the entry way wall a photo gallery of the family's happier days, pictures of them traveling in Europe, at the beach, at Mabel Lake in Canada where their family has had a small cabin for generations. I always found it sad to look at these pictures, especially the ones of Stu standing next to his plane. He loved the plane. It allowed him to fly into Mabel Lake and land on the water. Now it was an instrument of death.

Judy always tried to be generous around me, flowers from her garden, a cup of coffee, a glass of wine. We would find little things to be amused by—the new dachshund puppy, also known as sausage with paws, as it pathetically tried to climb the stairs chased by the Himalayan kitten I had given Kate. Now she had a dog that peed all over the kitchen floor instead of a husband. Our conversation felt like comrades in a combat trench extracting humor from our death watch. We'd share accounts of being dazed and misplacing things, crying in inappropriate places, fumbling and spilling. It didn't take much to amuse us.

When Kate would leave to do her homework, we'd sit at the table in the kitchen nook over our wine catching up on what was happening. It was odd how our lives were moving in opposite directions. Judy had been a nurse working part-time or on call, essentially at home with children. When Kate was on the mend, she took over the reins of the family business in the wood products industry. In the following months she became a busy executive and went on to run the small company while I, with the fast-lane career agenda, simply stopped in my tracks.

Time Warp

After the unveiling ceremony in which the headstone is laid by the grave, Judaism's marking of the end of the year of mourning, my ex-husband, Ivan, and I visited the cemetery together. He came to the house to pick me up. Being in the car with him was a time warp. All the body memories of his presence, the mannerisms, the quick-wittedness, the rushed staccato interactions, the way he rubbed his nose, were all still there. It was like turning back the clock, except that we were going on a date with death, and he was driving a Mercedes instead of a motorcycle.

It's a strange relationship with an ex-husband, the boy-man with whom I spent my youth, the man who fathered my only child. It was a tie that had been strained after our divorce, but his father's death and Elana's death within two months of each other brought us together. We

136

talked more in the last twelve months than we had in the last twelve years. Whatever our relationship had been, it was now something else.

Parking near the entrance, we solemnly got out of the car. A cemetery has its own form of tranquility, its own form of silence. The only sound was the wind in the trees and the call of a distant sparrow. I took the stillness in one nostril at a time. There was no need of dignity or decorum here where the dead speak through their silence and you can feel the sound of your own breath.

Elana's grave was next to the grave of Ivan's second son who died at three weeks from a congenital heart defect. There in the shadow of a huge, immaculately pruned chestnut tree sat two small matching rose granite headstones.

ELANA BESS GOLD
MARCH 1, 1975 -SEPTEMBER 29, 1991.
SHE WAS SPIRITED, SIXTEEN AND READY FOR LIFE
A PLANE CRASH TOOK HER IN AN INSTANT
MAY HER SOUL BE BOUND TO EVERLASTING LIFE

SIMON NAGEL GOLD
SEPTEMBER 21, 1986 - OCTOBER 12, 1986

Matching headstones. It's supposed to be matching twin beds, matching little coats or shoes, not matching gravestones. Having Elana's headstone match his other child's was very important to Ivan. At the time I had little emotion around his baby's death. It occurred many years ago when I had little generosity toward Ivan. Now seeing the matching headstones, I felt enormous compassion for his pain, for the heaviness in his heart for having put two children in the ground. We held each other for a long time, his lean torso towering over me, my face buried in his chest. Once united in marriage, forever united through death, my relationship with him felt strangely eternal. He was no longer ex-husband. He became my brother.

He sighed, I sighed; deep, helpless sighs. We walked back to the car arm in arm. We were the only ones there in the beginning and in the end—the circle of life you never expect to close around your children in your lifetime. Now, we would no longer be vying for precious time with her on the weekends. She would no longer be dividing her life between two families and two households. She would not be in our lives each day; but she is a presence when I am with Ivan. There is an unspoken sacredness between us now. All that went before does not matter—the divorce, the arguments about money, the anger—there is only the child we loved.

Step-Mothers

I have never been a step-mother. The closest I have come to knowing this daunting, much maligned role is being around Richard's children who are teenagers, hardly in need of another parent. But Elana had a step-mother from the time she was three, and Trudi was wonderful to her. Even after she had her own children, Elana was treated no differently from them. She gave her tea parties when she visited in the summers in San Francisco and brought her back pretty dresses from their travels. As Elana grew older, she allowed her to borrow clothes. Sometimes I wondered just how much of Trudi's wardrobe was in our house. We all wore the same size, Elana, Trudi, and I. It was an odd mix of feelings, an odd, but friendly relationship. Who knows what jealousies lie in the hearts of two women who have loved the same man.

Several times a week, my car would trace the familiar route to Trudi and Ivan's house to pick up or drop off Elana, or to retrieve a book, homework assignment, school paper, flute, or soccer shoe abandoned in her haste, but whose immediate importance had reached critical proportions. Up Broadway Drive, left on Myrtle, parking in front of the big house on the hill, toys on the porch, front door almost always open. Going inside, *Elana are you ready?* Matthew and Lauren, the two youngest of their three children running up and hugging me, always with something to show or tell while I waited for Elana. Sometimes I'd go up into her room to help her gather her things together. Invariably there would be an article of clothing, a book, a pair of shoes, or a piece of jewelry which I thought was long gone. She had this other life two days a week, the dimensions of which I was ever so slightly privy to when I'd wait for her inside their house.

Inside the house of an ex and his new wife. I was not quite a stranger, not quite a friend, a peculiar breed of relative. Dispossessed, gazing at the art which had hung on my walls, the couch which had graced my living room, the Wedgewood china which had been our wedding gift, now woven into the fabric of their life. I looked at the large David Hockney lithographs, the etched glass, the crystal chandelier, the motorcycles on the back patio, all the ways Ivan and I didn't fit given expression with another woman. It was a strange juxtaposition being in this house, like going back in time, but on an alien planet.

Trudi and Ivan are no longer married, but for all those years I usually made arrangements with Trudi. I miss not seeing her and the kids as I used to. Elana was the connection. She was very much a part of their life, the adored older sister, who was in and out, not there long enough to rouse the usual degree of sibling rivalries, there just enough to always be special.

Now when I run into Trudi on the street or at events, we exchange warm hugs. "How are you doing?"

"Okay."

"How are *you* doing?"

" Better." It is never an empty question.

"Let's have lunch or maybe we can go to the cemetery and plant new flowers around her grave."

Whether we are rushing to our cars laden with grocery bags or standing in a room full of people, we remind each other of Elana and it slices through the distractions of the moment like a whip. When we hug, our eyes tear, but it is a good sad. It is filled with love and makes us feel close. All the barriers of wife and ex-wife dissolve and I see only the best in her, her kindness, goodness, and generosity of heart. Sometimes I think Elana's death has opened the gates of heaven for the living.

Elana's Friends

Later that fall, I took Elana's best friends all out to lunch together. This was the first time we were all having lunch including Kate who was now able to get around on her own. They arrived together piling out of a shiny white Jeep Cherokee with a composure and self-assurance that hadn't been there before. Erika and Liz wore cute little mini skirts, Chessy and Kate in the casual baggy pant J. Crew look with long dangling earrings. I stepped back and looked at them like a distant auntie surveying the nieces she hasn't seen in a long time. These girls were becoming beautiful, mature, and alluring young women. It was hard to believe they were seventeen already. I know I embarrassed them when I ogled over how they had grown, but I couldn't help it. They were seniors in high school now. The milestone which marks adolescence and reshapes the psyche, left Elana behind. It was all I could do to stare at them in amazement.

I got out my camera and took their photograph. Peering at them through the wide angle lens as they stood in a line, I saw something different in their eyes, a distance, a sadness. I knew they were still friends, and I also knew they had struggled. The special camaraderie, the magic chemistry certain friendships acquire had been dislodged. You could see it in their stance. The pieces didn't fit together the same way without Elana, and the easy naturalness that was there before was gone. Now, here they were all together back in Elana's house. This time with Elana's mother in her place.

As we ate, we chatted about school, other friends and boyfriends. They all had had a very rough time most of this last year—difficulty concentrating at school, fearful and anxious, problems sleeping, not having the usual interest in things. Chessy showed me the essay for her college application. The theme was how Elana's death had left her questioning the meaning of life. "I don't know how you are supposed to be happy when it can all be over in an instant...what can you trust anymore." Liz confiding..."I think about Elana every day. Sometimes I imagine what it would be like if she were here instead of someone else...other times I get so angry she is gone that I yell at her and then I feel bad."

I was surprised how much they still thought about Elana, how much her death still affected them. But they were doing much better than the last time we had been together. The summer break had made it easier for them to face the long anticipated senior year without their best friend.

When we finished lunch, we promised to get together again. I knew we would. These four are very important to me, they are the way for my love for Elana to spill over to the living. I will always be there for them, they feel like my spiritual children. They are a big part of what remains of Elana's world. Keeping these ties alive is healing for us all.

Kate

Of all of them, Kate was the most changed. She was not the same person, even as more of her function returned. How could she be? She had encountered death and was lucky to be alive. Her father and best friend were dead. Even if she had no permanent brain damage, her life would never be the same. The adolescent illusion of immortality had been shattered. She had a deeper appreciation for what her peers took for granted. She was keenly aware of life's fragility and had become tentative in step and gait, out of sync with her friends who were partying, playing, and preparing for college. She was plucked out of the familiar world of a sixteen year-old and didn't know where she had been dropped.

I saw her more than the other girls. Staying in touch seemed important for both of us. I think we were both out of sync with our peers. She only lived a half-mile away and it was easy to find excuses to get together. "So Kate, come over for a latte and I'll show you the secret of getting perfect froth." It was something I might have said to Elana. We exchanged a big warm hug as she got out of the car. She was wearing khaki shorts and hiking boots. Her perfectly smooth tanned legs revealed only a small scar on the side of the thigh. Slowly we walked arm in arm to the front door. "How are you doing Katie, honey?"

Sigh, "Okay."

"What's the matter?"

"I'm nervous about a history test. I have to read the material a hundred times to remember anything. It takes me forever. I'm stressed out about school all over again and I'm only attending two classes."

I had an idea. After our coffee, I asked Kate if she would be interested in a little hypnosis to help her relax about the test. A teenager at heart, mind altering phenomenon had an appeal. She sat back in the big easy chair and closed her eyes. Poor Katie, she had lost her confidence. I would help her remember her successes, taking her back through the challenges in her life to review how she had successfully met them. Leading her into deeper and deeper states of relaxation, asking her to go back and remember the very first hard thing she had ever faced...

When we finished and she opened her eyes, her face seemed softer. We sat quietly and let it all sink in. "That was neat, I feel better." Later she called and told me she handled the test well. I was glad to be able to help her in some small way, but fundamentally Kate was struggling. You could see how misplaced she felt, how depressed under the veneer of trying to be okay. The spark was gone, the easy laugh and natural smile were labored. She was very lonely. Everything she did took a long time, from going up the stairs to reading the directions on a can of soup. But Kate was determined. She had been an excellent student and hard-driving athlete. If anyone could make it, I knew she could.

Traces

One evening we were having dinner with Richard's children at a Chinese restaurant to celebrate his daughter Dorothea's fourteenth birthday. Hunched over steaming bowls of egg drop soup, Aaron and Dorothea playfully teased each other about various aspects of their newly-acquired and tentatively-held maturity now that she was a freshman and he was a senior. I was flooded with memories of the last time we were at this restaurant with Elana, an insignificant evening by any other standards. Aaron and Dorothea were still giggles and spills while Elana and Chessy, fidgeting with the car keys, lobbied to go next door to the jewelry store to get a second pierce in their ears. After a discussion appropriate to the flagging parental authority over such matters, they ran off while we waited for dessert, returning triumphant five minutes later, each with one green stud above their silver hoops. Delighted at the success of their lobbying efforts and the fact that they convinced the clerk to split the piercing fee between them, a familial merriment filled the air. Now two years later, Dorothea was interjecting her brand of logic on the subject of double, even triple, piercing—but I was remembering Elana. I couldn't share the anecdote because it would have spoiled the celebratory atmosphere. Richard's children seemed uncomfortable if I talked about Elana. Occasionally, I would tell an anecdote just to break the ice, so she wouldn't become an unmentionable, but it always felt unnatural.

143

Elana's death sat silently in the middle of everything we did together, from festive dinners at restaurants to driving to the mountain to ski. I hid my tears around them, but my mood was always subdued. None of us knew how to talk about it. I knew her death made them sad, but this was not a shared loss. We were not a biological family, not even a step-family. Their schools and worlds had been quite separate from Elana's, and though they liked each other and had had their share of family outings and vacations with Elana, they had not been close. I think Richard's children didn't know how to react to me after the accident. Over a year later, it was still very difficult to talk about our feelings. Frankly, for all my professional training, I wasn't much help.

Brazil

As the winter rains descended, I got better at daily functioning, mastering the perfunctory and necessary, but this was not where my heart was. The secret world of the mourner is the real world, the face that people see is not the real face. The hunger to find my place in the world and meaning in Elana's death was still the deepest resonance of my life. But now I knew better than to fret or coax the universe. I simply waited to see what would unfold.

One day, I received information in the mail about a study trip to Brazil focusing on non-traditional healers and visits to esoteric spiritual centers. This trip, led by a well known scholar, would immerse us in a culture where people of all faiths and strata of society participated in Spiritist sects and believed in communication with the spirit world. I still had money left in Elana's college account and this was an incredible opportunity to experience things not accessible to the ordinary tourist. So off I went, March 1, 1993—the day she would have been eighteen, the age of emancipation. I could not even conceive of letting her go.

The trip began in Sao Paulo with a visit to one of the many Spiritist centers, the Temple Garcia, to participate in an Umbanda ritual in which Afro-Brazilian gods are channeled. Arriving at a small white church, a very ordinary Christian edifice with a large cross on the top, we climbed the steep marble steps leading to a narrow portal. Inside hundreds of people were lined up around the periphery of the sanctuary waiting to be healed. Statues of both Christian saints and African deities stood next to each other on the dais. Off to the left, where the pulpit would have been, four drummers sat on stools behind large colorful African drums, and the priestess dressed in a simple white gown bowed in the center ready to begin.

The drummers placed their hands on their drums and tapped a soft, lingering beat. A hush came over the room. The priestess raised her arms to the heavens and began to gracefully dance in circles, swaying her arms rhythmically above her head. Soon her eyes closed, the drumming intensified and her dancing and singing became more rapturous. Twenty or thirty mediums clad in white began filing into the room twirling and calling to the spirits until the center of the sanctuary was a mass of white movement. The drumming built to a crescendo as the mediums, now in ecstatic trance, whirled fervishly around the center of the brightly lit room. Tonight they were channeling Caboclo spirits, ancestral spirits of Indian cults.

Our group stood on the sidelines watching with the others who had come for healing when suddenly there was a surge of power coming from the center of the sanctuary that forced us to step back. One by one the mediums began crying out in guttural tones, lighting cigars and pounding their chests as their bodies jerked and twitched. Some of them put on Indian headdresses. They squinted their eyes and their faces became contorted. The spirits were ready to work. The people who were waiting were quickly

145

ushered into the center to individual mediums who performed hands-on healing while assistants took notes and wrote down "prescriptions." The room became hot and filled with cigar smoke as the mesmerizing beat of the drums reverberated to dizzying heights. There were sick children, old people, well dressed men from the city. The mediums worked at a frenetic pace for several hours as the huge lines of people waiting for healing were whisked into the center of the sanctuary.

Finally it was our turn. I was led to a rather heavy woman with long coarse hair and a cigar hanging from her mouth. She had a powerful countenance and dark piercing eyes that seemed to look right through you. Maggie, our translator, simply told her that my daughter had died. Without blinking, she began rapidly moving her hands over the magnetic field around my body, making larger and larger sweeping movements. She continued moving her arms wildly, uttering strange incantations, her eyes far away focused on something only she could see. It felt as if she were communicating with Elana.

"Maggie," I asked, "What is she doing? Is Elana here? Is there a dark illness in me that she sees?"

"I don't know, all I told her was that you were sad for your daughter."

The medium continued her frenetic sweeping movements, alternately pounding herself on the chest and uttering unintelligibly. Sweat poured down her face. She looked possessed. I stood transfixed, willingly accepting whatever magical powers she wielded. I was so bereft in my own culture of doctoring for the soul that whatever catharsis or cleansing, whatever healing lay at the root of this ancient practice, I gratefully received. When she was finished she took the cigar out of her mouth and through glazed eyes spoke to the translator. She said she had done a healing for my daughter so she could move to a higher realm. She must be allowed to go further on her way and I must let her go. This must happen so there is less sadness and I can start to be happy again. She told me only to think of the good memories, and to lie in a bath and rub a paste of coarse salt over my body to cleanse my spirit. The assistant wrote this out on a pad along with a prescription to pray over white candy and a glass of water to help me heal.

I thanked the healer and went back to stand with the group. I felt light headed and confused. I came here to learn how to be closer to Elana. I was being told to let her go.

Strange Phenomenon

We met with other "sensitifs" and gifted healers, people who had left traditional professions because they had been "called" and who channeled other intelligent entities who could allegedly cure disease and cancers or communicate with the dead. At one such center in the capital, Brasilia, we were introduced to a man who was considered an extraordinary "sensitif." The leader of our group was very interested in meeting with this man for research purposes. We were having lunch with him at the university cafeteria when someone noticed that small stones began to drop to the floor near his table. Suddenly everyone rushed over to the table where our guest was sitting because stigmata, the three points on the skin which bleed in the manner of Christ's wounds, had just manifested in the palm of his hand. In near disbelief, we asked him about the stones and the stigmata. He said that he has periods of heightened psychic sensitivity, as did his father and grandfather and, now, his son. During these times many phenomena occur including the ability to materialize objects, heal, and travel out of his body.

This was more than I could fathom, but as we walked outside to go to the conference room, more stones seemed to just drop to the ground. Someone gave him a white agate that she saw bounce to the ground and asked him about it. He held it in his hand and closed his eyes. When he opened his hand there were two identical white agates in the palm of his hand. He explained when this phenomenon occurs there is a cinnamon odor in his hands. And indeed there was. Fairly incredulous, but quite convinced because we were standing right next to him, suddenly everyone in the group was handing him agates and besieging him with questions.

I patiently waited my turn and handed him an aquamarine ring that I had purchased on the trip because it was Elana's birth stone. I asked him if he could tell me anything about her death or if he could communicate with her. He closed his eyes and held the ring in his hand and said, "She died on the weekend, didn't she?"

"Yes, it was a Sunday," I responded.

He looked at me with soft melting eyes full of compassion, and said that she was meant to come through like a comet, her time here was not meant to be long. When a child dies on the weekend, in their culture, that child is said to be in her "last afternoon", meaning that her work is complete and she does not have to return to the physical plane. He said she knew she was leaving. He held my hand and looked me deep in the eyes and told me to think about the privilege of having had her and to help unfortunate children here in Brazil and at home, that this would help us both. Then as if he could read my mind, he said, "You will learn much about her death in Brazil."

In Recife in northern Brazil, the heart of the Afro-Brazilian culture, we met with a respected Candoble priest/healer. We convened in the basement of his makeshift church where life-sized statues of the Orixas, powerful African deities, lined the walls. He was kind enough to offer to read our chakras, telling us where our energy was blocked and where physical problems could be developing. He worked very fast, sensing with his hands then telling the person what he saw, and moving on to the next person. People were fairly stunned by the accuracy of what he said. When he got to me, he jumped back suddenly and began to frantically whisk his hands all around my body

148

exclaiming, "There is the spirit of a dead person around you, it is not good." Everyone in our group came running over as he continued this frenzied motion imploring the spirit to leave. I stood there immobilized. Finally, I said it was my daughter, and I didn't want her to go. He looked into my eyes intensely, paused and said slowly, deliberately, and with authority, "It is not good for her, you must let her go." I felt as if I had been punched in the chest. I couldn't possibly let her go, it was too soon, I would disintegrate if I lost my connection to her. Why was he telling me this? It's not right. Barely able to speak, I asked the burning question, "Won't she come to help me from the other side?"

His reply was soft, "It is not good for you to call her to you in your grieving. This is her journey, not yours. She will come to you and help you if that is her mission."

Wherever we were given the opportunity to work with the healers, I asked about Elana, about why she died, if they could communicate with her, if she was trying to communicate with me. Time and again, I was told that Elana is happy and is in the light and that, most of all, I needed to let her go. At the very last opportunity, I implored a Brazilian shaman to please tell me if there is a way I can "really" communicate with her. In broken English, she told me that Elana is the energy of pure love, that she exists as a different vibration, and that when I open my heart to pure love, I will be on the same vibration. I didn't know what she was talking about. These words were New Age spiritual abstractions to me. Then I remembered Kate's near-death experience and her words as she emerged from coma, "Elana is pure love, she is pure heart."

Brazil left me confused. Why was I always being told to let her go? What I sought was knowledge about why she had died. Was she an old soul, had she been here before, was her time meant to be brief? Would this have been her destiny regardless of my decision to allow her to fly? Rationally, I understood that beliefs about death are culture bound, but on another level, I must have thought there was absolute knowledge about her death and eventually I would find it and instinctively recognize its truth. I must have thought I would find someone who could indisputably communicate with her, leaving me no doubt about her soul's existence.

I left Brazil realizing for the very first time that I may never know whether Elana's death was a random accident or whether it was her "time." I may never know whether her last words were the insolent angry teenager speaking or the wisdom of a higher self who knew. I was now left facing myself. How was I going to reconcile my decision to allow her to fly, how was I going to forgive myself?

Speaking in Dreams

Shortly after I returned from Brazil, I had a powerful dream in which Elana came home. She came not as a character but as the sense of presence I described in the dreams I called visitations. She hugged me and sat on my lap just as she did as a child. The sweetness of having her near once more and enjoying the simple pleasure of her company was palpable. *Oh, Elana, I'm so glad you are here. I miss you so much. My life is now the way it should be.* I floated in an immeasurable ecstasy, a sublime ephemeral reality where death can be undone. Elana is back, all that has been wrong has been righted. I danced around the house, my heart filled with a joy I hadn't known since her birth. But there was a strange sense of something pulling on her, a sense that she might not be able to stay with us. It was an ominous "force" or energy. I decided to take action. I wasn't helpless. I would take her to have this force, this energy that was drawing her away, exorcized. Yes, that would be the best solution. Then she could stay. *Elana, let's go. Hurry up. We can fix this.* Just as we were about to get in the car to go to have it exorcized, the dream ended and I woke up.

I lay in bed thinking, was she being pulled away by the forces of her destiny? Was that it...was that what I was being told in Brazil...that I can't hold her. This is a force I can't exorcize. I can't hold her against her own destiny, I have to let her go. Did she now come in the dream to tell me that herself?

Having to Tell People

The second spring arrived with the budding of pink camellias and the scent of pine forests coming alive. Time was now marked in relation to her death. I was out in the world more. Sometimes it was all right, sometimes it wasn't. One night at a reception I ran into an old acquaintance, someone I had known in my single years. In the eight years since we had seen each other she had married and had three children. She had achieved the dreams which at age thirty-five when I knew her were becoming elusive.

She enthusiastically asked about my daughter, whom she imagined must be in high school by now. My heart began to pound, I could feel the blood draining from my face. Having to tell someone who knew you then, when life's grand plan was in your hands, when there was naive hope and positive expectation about the future, when men were the topic of conversation, was like receiving the mortal blow all over again.

"So how *is* your daughter?" she repeated. The contrast between the innocence of the question, the unsuspecting optimism in her face and the brutal truth, made telling her even more difficult. I looked away, my eyes welling up. There I was, no sunglasses, exposed, trapped in the middle of a room of people gaily bantering and clicking wine glasses. I could lie, I thought, then make a quick escape before she could ask any more questions. I couldn't move. I opened my mouth but the words wouldn't come. My throat tightened and every vein in my neck pulsated as I fought back emotion. Taking a sip of wine, trying to swallow, "...she...um...there...um...there was a plane crash last year...." The horror-struck look on her face, the "Oh my God," that hushed the chattering of those standing near us, it was like reliving the moment when everything in my life changed.

I was debilitated by the encounter. The lifeblood went out of me for that entire weekend. I grieved as I did in the beginning, teary, sad, immobilized. It is like this. Just when you start to get used to the new reality of your life, an innocent event carries you full force back to the very depths of your loss.

Even as we heal and step back into the flow of life, grief remains the crosscurrent, full of riptides and eddies. Some pull you in unsuspecting; others you see coming.

High School Graduation

Milestones open the grave. It was a weekend I dreaded. I pretended there were no proud and ecstatic teenagers lining up in black robes in stadiums across the country, no parents with tear stained cheeks straining to catch a glimpse of their progeny from crowded bleachers. The calling of names, the handing of the diploma, this erstwhile rite of passage, all of Elana's hard work for nothing.

I was incapable of attending the graduation ceremony for Richard's son or for Elana's classmates, but on Sunday I managed to drop by the open house at both Kate's and Erika's. It was one of those perfect June days, glorious sunshine, a cloudless blue sky, a reason in and of itself to feel celebratory. I drove the half mile to Kate and Judy's house, parked at the bottom of the driveway and sat unable to command my hand to pull the door handle. I finally climbed out and walked up the path to the front entrance. I could hear the laughing voices inside. Deep sigh. I don't know if I can do this. Kate came to the door wearing a short white sheath and high-heeled patent leather pumps. The radiance of her smile melted the knot in my stomach. A warm embrace, "how lovely and svelte you look, Katie, congratulations." She was a miracle in motion. Pride radiated. It was contagious.

It was a small intimate gathering, family and a few close friends. I was talking with two of the girls who were on the soccer team with Elana about where they were going to college when someone proposed a toast. Glasses raised, all eyes were on Kate. She was beaming. She looked like her old self. The school had permitted her to graduate with her class pending completion of the necessary credits at the community college. That she had been able to join her class and do any of the work at all was an extraordinary accomplishment. Judy stood looking at Kate forcing back the tears as the weight of all they had been through sliced through the joy of the moment. When Judy started to cry, tears streamed down my face. We walked toward each other and embraced. All eyes were on us. Two mothers, one graduation.

I left after that and drove to Erika's. There was a large crowd on the back deck drinking and laughing. A barbecue was going and food and drink were being lavishly bestowed on the guests. The atmosphere was very festive. I tried to be sociable. Terribly self-conscious, I could feel that everyone knew who I was. I was the mother of Erika's best friend who died in that plane crash. I was Elana's stand-in, a painful reminder of our fragility, the face of death in the midst of celebration. The air was thick with this awareness, but no one said a word.

I retreated to a corner table, sipping champagne with Chessy's mother Francie, and Liz's parents, Doug and Susan, who were at the airport with the girls when the plane crashed. I tried to make small talk. It was difficult watching her friends and classmates as they bantered gaily, all dressed up in ties and jackets and linen dresses, composed, graceful, more mature than I had remembered.

As I was getting ready to leave, Erika's father who

was standing with a group of guests, grabbed me in a big teddy bear hug. Towering above me, his arm protectively gripping my shoulder, he looked us all in the eye, his voice cracking as he started to speak, "We think about Elana all the time. We can't pretend this didn't happen, we can't make it an unmentionable. She was like part of the family to us and we miss her, especially today."

A hush came over the group. Eyes of strangers brimmed with tears. No one stirred. I was so grateful to Dan Kinney for breaking the silence. It was an act of courage to speak of something so frightening and painful and stir the emotions we all felt. Even though my eyes watered in front of people I didn't know, it was an enormous relief. People are so afraid of emotion, but it was the only honest thing to do.

Going into Her Room

I thought I would be able to change her room now that she would have been graduating from high school and leaving for college. It had been a year and a half. I found I could no more dismantle the blue and white flowered Laura Ashley motif, give away the remains of her closet, remove the representative assortment of T-shirts from her drawers than I could move a mountain, or would want to.

I recalled the forbidden room at the end of the hall on the second floor of my grandmother's house in Philadelphia. A dark mahogany door with a small window above it was the first thing you saw as you reached the top of a long creaky staircase. This door was always closed. No one spoke about it. I never saw anyone go inside. All I was told was that it had been my grandfather's room and as a child I thought his ghost must be in there. This quarantined corner cast a powerful aura, leaving my imagination to conjure sinister spells and creatures with long spindly legs. I was brave enough to occasionally look through the keyhole, but all that I could ever see were the dusty old floorboards. Lured by the forbidden, I sometimes put my hand on the doorknob, turned it ever so slightly until it squeaked, then jumped back terrified, and ran down the stairs, never saying a word. It wasn't until I was in junior high school and the house was being sold that the door was opened and I finally saw what was inside. It was a large grey bedroom with twin beds, a maple dresser, rocking chair, rug, and some pictures on the wall. No ghosts, witches, or spider webs draping the faded walls. I don't think anything had been touched in over a decade.

I go into Elana's room to remember, to be with her, to look for pieces of her I missed the last time I was in there. Sometimes I just sit on her bed hoping she will come. I stare at the mementos on her bulletin board, the sports medals, concert ticket stubs, soccer team photos and party invitations. I touch the earring collection carefully strung on the wall. I try on her make-up and perfumes, I borrow a purse or ribbon hanging in the corner. I open the closet and try to remember how she looked in the red jean skirt. I can even remember the fish mobile hanging over her crib, the yellow and white bunny wallpaper, the changing table that sat in the corner with the stack of diapers and tub of pop-up baby wipes.

Her room is like a womb, a sacred container that holds her presence from beginning to end. It exudes her being. It draws me toward it like a magnetic pole. Even though I know the pain that comes with entering what has become death's den, I cannot stay out. Her room still has a life force. I'm not ready to give it up. I don't care if it appears that I am clinging to the past. Grief doesn't have a clock. As I have given away treasured possessions to her friends, I regret the dwindling material evidence of her life. I've kept an assortment of her clothing, jewelry, shoes, books, and tapes because they all have a story about what they meant to her. When I look at them I remember how we were together. Without them, I might forget.

I don't think there should be "a supposed to" about

preserving or changing someone's room after they have died. The memories that live in these rooms need to be tended as they direct us. Neither too much nor too little attachment is good. Rooms will dismantle themselves when they are ready.

Stolen Moments

August 26, my birthday, almost two years since the accident. It is getting easier to breathe. Richard and I were out to dinner with a few close friends enjoying the superb food and reminiscing about the old days. High on the wine, cuisine, and company, I felt like my old self. *Remember how we met...you were going out with what's her name, no, no you were going out with what's his name, no no...it was...Yeah, but remember Loey's famous chocolate party with the chocolate dipped Nike running shoe as the center-piece and the New York party with the chopped liver sculpture of the Empire State Building...Remember when we all ran the Cascade Run Off, and what about the time we waited for Bruce Springsteen at the Benson Hotel until four in the morning...and then the time....*
What is it about the good old days that makes them so good? Whatever it was, these reminiscences were working their magic. Reveling in the antics of the past, I still had hold of who I had been. I felt glad to be alive. The waiter arrived with a plate of exquisitely prepared salmon on a bed of purple radicchio dotted with colorful slivers of carrots and beets and rich creamy mushroom risotto and placed it in front of me. Next a sliced duck breast, Cajun crab cakes, lamb in gooseberry sauce. Each dish more enticing than the last. *What a feast. More champagne for everyone!* At that moment life was good. For the first time in two years, I was thoroughly enjoying myself. Suddenly, out of nowhere, the sadness of missing Elana crashed over

me. Like an unexpected breaker in a calm sea, it came without warning in a stolen moment when life felt bountiful.

I think it is always there bidding in the back of my mind whenever I lose myself and slip into the spirit of things. *How can you have such a good time,* the voice says, *Elana's not here. This exuberance is not reality. Your daughter is dead.* My chest caves in, my head falls, the magic of the moment is gone. Rationally I know that I am not betraying Elana's memory by feeling good. She would not want me to be suffering. But once the spell is broken, it is broken, and a self-consciousness lingers on to instruct me to enjoy my birthday.

Grief's journey has taught me that joy and sorrow, sadness and pleasure can co-exist. They have to. One does not negate the other although it feels that way for a long time. And when pleasure grows to outweigh the pain, that is as it should be.

Euphemisms

The dreaded question. Standing at a political gathering, making small talk. "Do you have children?" The query always begins innocently enough. "None at home," or "I lost a child in an accident," or "My only child was in a fatal plane crash at the age of sixteen." Lost, gone, departed, perished, not at home—anything but dead. Euphemisms don't soften the blow for the questioner, but for me they do.

After all this time, I still can't say the words, "Elana is dead." It is like being hit head-on, a pronouncement I don't need to be reminded of, an image too graphic for a mother to behold. *Elana is dead.* Subject, verb, object. It sounds a false absolute. The words too exacting, cold, and compressed to describe the unrevealed mysterious vastness of the other side of life. It is an objective truth, but so

157

far from the experience that its ring hurts the ear. *ELANA IS DEAD.* Not true, protests the voice inside. Death is not so simple. It is not clinical denial. It is more than getting away from the scathing harshness of the words, from having death's seeming definitiveness thrown in your face. These are our children, our blood line, guts, and heart are with them, and they remain with us. A part of them does not die. Death does not end our relationship with them. It changes it. How can I say, "Elana is dead," when so much of her spirit surrounds me?

Home from the meeting, I sit at my kitchen table staring out the window as dusk approaches. I force myself to say the words over and over just to see why they are so hard to say, to see if I can desensitize myself, to see if I can make myself face death's frontal view. *Elana is dead, Elana is dead, ELANA IS DEAD.* I want to take a two by four and whirl around and in one lightening movement smash everything in sight. It is a rage that blind sides me, a scream that echoes into the night, even now. NOT DEAD, NOT DEAD, NOT ELANA. Not the whole truth. No wonder I can't say the words. They awaken the sleeping demons.

She is gone. That feels better. I can say that.

It Gets Better

I remember in the beginning people who lost children saying to me, "It gets better." I wondered what "it" was. What exactly gets better? I didn't understand what they meant, I couldn't imagine the pain ever going away, but I took it on faith.

Now, I too, can say I am healing. Losing Elana shattered the ground on which I stood, casting me far outside ordinary wants and desires, away from the ego's domain and a new alignment was taking over. I was closer to being just who I was, nothing to prove, nothing to hide, no agendas to push, a new level of authenticity and self-acceptance carved from the uninvited study of impermanence.

I no longer plead to have her back. I no longer get sucked into a vortex of pain that spins me around and releases me into a void. Weeks go by without shedding a tear. I miss Elana and always will. I still cry for her, but the wound left by her being so suddenly and fiercely wrenched from me is softening.

At first, I was discomfited by the absence of the searing grief which was how I felt connected to Elana. In its absence I feel more disconnected from her. My grief for her and her presence through that grief was all there was for a long time. I was afraid I was being disloyal if I wasn't in pain. In some ways, I feel further away from her, and in other ways I know she is always with me. My search for her has been on the outside, looking to the spirit world. I am beginning to see that perhaps she is to be found within.

Mourning is a necessary retreat from the world. Grief is an inward journey. It is its own form of coma, a half-alive state, a slow, unsteady re-emergence. In the movie *Forrest Gump*, after Jenny his beloved dies, Forrest starts running, all day every day, month after month, with no destination or goal, a rhythmic movement to remain in this world, but not part of it, running without reason for three years until he didn't need to anymore. Then he came home. Ann Morrow Lindbergh writing about the kidnaping and death of her son speaks of the urge to follow, how like Orpheus we try to follow the dead on the beginning of their journey, but like Orpheus, we can't go all the way, and after a long journey we come back. If we are lucky, we are reborn.

The journey into the underworld has no form. It has no destination. Each one who returns lights the way for others.

PART V: The Mending of a Broken Heart

*"If I keep a green bough in my heart,
the singing bird will come."*

...Chinese proverb

A Modern Day Lourdes

In the spring of 1994, two and a half years after the accident, I decided to take a one month sabbatical from work. On March 1, Elana's birthday, I was on a Singapore Airlines jet on my way to Bali. This was now my third journey on her birthday, first to Esalen in Big Sur, California, then Brazil, now Bali. I think I was looking to be born again.

Some people would say to me, oh how lucky you are to be going to Bali. I felt like saying, oh how lucky you are, none of your children are dead. How quickly they forget. These journeys were not vacations, well deserved respites from ordinary trials and tribulations. These trips were like going to Lourdes, hoping for the miracle that would finally put my broken life back together.

I closed my eyes as the huge jet lifted off the runway. Nineteen years ago at this time, 6:30 a.m., I had just begun labor. It lasted all day. When it was over, I was handed this little bundle of wrinkles and squeaks that I would come to love more than anything else. Sixteen years—that is all the time I was given. Gazing out the window at the vastness of the unchanging scape of grey matter that this womblike vessel mysteriously penetrates, I knew she was out there somewhere.

It's good to be on a plane when you are sad. You can't get up and so easily distract yourself. There is total anonymity in a cargo of 450 people stacked neatly in rows like canned goods. As I looked around, I wondered about the stories contained within the mass of nodding heads huddled under the industrial blue blankets. Mothers and suckling babies, grandmothers, grandfathers, fathers and children. Family fragments. I took comfort in the knowledge that amongst these mostly Asian people were many who had undoubtedly lost family. After all, Singapore was a hub airport for Southeast Asia, for Vietnam. I wondered how many were going home, and to what. I knew on this plane I was not alone in suffering, but part of a much larger story.

Soon I was sitting on the balcony of a little hotel in the middle of an emerald rice paddy surrounded by lush tropical palms, watching women with straw hats hunched over canals doing the laundry. In the morning a breakfast of artfully presented fresh fruit, yoghurt, and pancakes was served by houseboys in colorful sarongs as the gentle strains of the gamelan echoed from behind the garden wall. Sometimes in English and sometimes in Balinese, always in a singsong voice and an engaging smile, "Selemat pagi, goot morning."

"Good morning, Katut, Selemat pagi, Yoman."

"You are learning to speak good Balinese."

"You are learning good English."

"Did you sleep well? You like your breakfast? Can I get you something else?"

Their smiles ignited the cold places in my heart. These were village people, the warmth of their smiles, their friendliness and helpfulness bore the authenticity of the Balinese character. It wasn't something they learned in hotel school. Each greeting, each smile expressed a genuine warmth of spirit. It was contagious. My heart began to smile.

We took a trip to Besakih, the mother temple of all Bali, which sits high on the slopes of the Gunung Agung volcano. We drove narrow twisted roads through primordial tropical forests, past phosphorescent rice fields cascading down mountainsides, and into villages where women in bright sarongs bearing magnificent offerings of fruit mounded high upon their heads gathered at the temple gates. I stopped to photograph the silhouette of a lone farmer with his oxen plowing his field in a neon valley. Wherever we turned, we were surrounded by vistas of luminescent green as far as the eye could see. It was beyond breathtaking. It was the lure of beauty that leaves you speechless. It came into my cells and carried me far outside grief's reach.

As our little group arrived at Besakih, the skies opened up and the rains poured down. We climbed the several hundred steps to the temple undeterred, arriving at a large open pavilion where offerings are left and where you can receive the blessing of the temple priest. Perched in the clouds in this most sacred of all temples, we sat on our knees in a line, sarongs tucked tightly beneath our ankles, eyes closed in prayer, as an old Hindu priest dressed in white muslin came down the line and blessed each of us with holy water.

Even though Bali has been changed by tourism, some would say ruined, there remain places of unspoiled beauty and serenity. It took me back in time, away from the modern world. I experienced a rhythm, a way of life we can't access in Western culture. I soaked up everything it had to show me, from the women who appeared each morning bent down in prayer leaving small offerings at the entrance to the family compound to the tranquil rhythms of the gamelan. I wandered through the little artisan villages, sitting for hours on grass mats visiting with the craftsman and watching them work. I ran through the monkey forest and sat by the ancient banyan tree sharing my bananas with a family of monkeys. I bought tinctures and salves as the old woman in the market eager to be helpful tried in sign language to explain their many uses. I had wonderful massages from a young Indonesian girl who would bring a hard boiled egg and strong lemon tea and sweetly intone "Goot, goot, you like? Eat, It's goot for you."

A Spirit Meeting with Elana

Toward the end of the trip, we went to meet with a traditional healer, called a Balian Taksu, who specialized in channeling spirits from the other side. We drove down a rocky dirt road, scattering chickens as we came to the family compound where the healer lived. We were led inside through several sparsely furnished rooms to a courtyard. Past the goats, laundry drying in the sun, gingerly stepping over rows of squash and turnips, a baby pig crossing our path, we were brought to a small concrete pavilion. The Balian, who was also a priestess, sat on a straw mat behind a raised altar. She wore a beautiful white sarong, her dark hair piled high on her head. Candles and Balinese incense were burning and pictures of Hindu deities hung on the wall. We gave her our "offering," a specially prepared basket of food and money. All that was said was that I was the person wanting help. She began chanting and praying and went into trance. Then she held her stomach, moaning about not being able to eat, making gestures of vomiting. She spoke about how I should get married and what to do with a gift of money. I immediately knew my mother who had died of stomach cancer six years earlier had come through. The priestess conveyed the exact conditions of my mother's illness and last days, and relayed questions and concerns that my mother and I had discussed before her death. I was astounded by all this, even amused. My mother was still worried about whether I would get remarried, even now.

But I wanted to speak with Elana, so the translator asked if we could speak with my daughter. Immediately the woman began crying about a big explosion in the sky and falling to the earth, how it was all so sudden and unexpected. The translation was sporadic in between sobs about her missing me and being so sorry. But, the staccato breathless sobs, words sputtering on the inhale, and heaving chest was exactly how Elana cried. It sounded like her, it felt like her. The pain expressed was enormous, so real that I began to cry also. I asked if Elana was "really" here, if I could talk to her directly. The priestess gave

166

me an urn of holy water and told me to spill it three times and call her name. *"Elana, Elana, please come, do you have a message for me?"* My eyes were riveted on the Balian. She stopped crying. There was an odd thickness in the air. She spoke calmly and definitively and said Elana wanted me to have a boyfriend and to be happy. She didn't want me to be alone and sad and missing her.

What a short message, I thought. Why didn't Elana tell me something more interesting? It wasn't until later that I realized how serious her message was. Elana knew that my greatest loyalty, and the deepest love I have is for her. She was giving permission and wanting me to give that love to Richard. Even at her urging, I don't think I can ever love anyone the way I loved her.

Once again I had an emotional experience trying to communicate with Elana through a medium from another culture. As we drove out of the compound, I kicked myself for not having the presence of mind to ask something only Elana could have known, something that might have provided more evidence that this was really her. I forgot to ask if there were messages for her friends, her father, her brothers or sister. I did ask if it was Elana's "time" and the Balian said "No, no, it was an accident, Elana was an innocent, it was not her time." This contradicted what the healers in Brazil said. But now I understood that I can never prove the validity of these experiences. The fact that they are helpful emotionally is enough.

The day before my departure, I was eating lunch in the small open air-restaurant at the edge of the rice field, gazing out at the luminescence for the last time. I surveyed the marvelous masks and shadow puppets on the walls. I thought about why I was so drawn to this exotic place; why we are drawn to certain cultures, to certain experiences, be they by the sea, deep in the forest, or in a foreign land. Does the psyche intuitively recognize what it needs to restore balance? Does our soul's yearning draw us toward things before they enter the conscious mind? Why did I come here? What did I expect from this trip?

That evening, I sat out on my balcony in the moon-light. Bathed by a balmy breeze I still pondered the question of what this journey was about. It hadn't brought spiritual revelation, it hadn't brought insight into what my life should be now. This was my last chance for revelation. I stood up and went over to the edge of the balcony and looked out at a sky ablaze with stars, "Oh, Elana, oh ancient ones in this magical place, if you are out there, please answer me." I went back and sat on the edge of the railing with my knees tucked under my chin quietly taking in my last night in this enchanted land. Slowly the crickets in the rice field below began to chirp. Their chorus grew louder and louder until their song filled the night air. "Are you singing for me?" I asked in wonder and awe. When they were done, the night once again became silent.

It was difficult to leave Bali. The rhythm of life resonated with something that was awakening within, a new order of experience, a new order of priorities that I longed to know. It took me away from the frantic rush of modern life. It nourished my soul. I left Bali still trying to figure out what would heal my broken heart, all the while not realizing it was already on the mend.

Planting a Rose Garden

When I returned from Bali, I went to work on turning an unsightly corner of the back yard into a memorial rose garden for Elana. The previous summer a friend and I had driven to a grower about an hour from Portland to order the plants. When we arrived, we feasted our eyes on seemingly endless fields of roses, all in bloom. We trudged out past the barns and greenhouses in the hot sun to the eastern field. The very first row we came upon was a silky pale yellow rose named ELINA. Chills went down my spine, out of the hundreds of varieties which dotted these fields, what led us to this one. It was as if the universe was answering...*Elana is pleased about your rose garden for her*. And as we walked up and down every row carefully smelling each variety making a meticulous list of the most beautiful and fragrant, white butterflies visited.

Steve High, my landscaper, came over to help me plant the rose garden. It was his gift to me, a Saturday afternoon to plant a rose garden for my daughter. This was a sacred project, nothing more needed to be said. He brought over special compost from his own yard and the loving intention that surrounded our work gave us both solace. We dug sixteen large holes. Kneeling over each one, almost as if in prayer, I mixed in the peat moss and compost with my bare hands. With a blessing, I set each plant in place. The raging tears that watered the two rose bushes I planted right after she died were gone.

When we were finished, we stood back and looked at the bare canes artistically placed amongst large rocks and mounds. The rose named ELINA was in the center. I wedged a memorial plaque engraved with Elana's drawing of The Grateful Dead's Dancing Bear at the entrance. It says "Have a Grateful Day" and brings a smile to my face, for I know this is what Elana would be saying now.

I meander through the garden every day in the summer, just to be there and smell the roses. I find peace amongst these flowers. Their beauty overwhelms me. The ambrosia of their fragrance and the magnificence of their bloom appearing anew each spring continue to be like miracles to me. Sometimes when I close my eyes, I can see Elana dancing amongst the flowers. I think the rose divas have heard my tears.

Leaving a Mark

I drove up to the mountains in early June for the second gathering of Elana's memorial environmental project. Blasting her favorite music, latte in hand, the hot

169

sun radiating through the windshield, I imagined her sitting in the seat beside me bouncing to the rhythms of Bob Marley. I was glad to be doing this. It was comforting to return to the now familiar back roads, Forest Service road 4810, past Beaver Creek, the vista that opens at the Tygh Valley turnoff. It was comforting to be building a tradition, a week in the Mt. Hood National Forest with a group of highly committed and energetic teachers and students. We have come to feel a deep bond to our adopted site, seeing the endangered redband trout return and the willows planted along the stream bed growing. The forest rangers who work with us every day are very appreciative, often amazed that students can work so hard and accomplish so much.

Elana's friends did not participate this year, they were off at college or other jobs, but when I arrived I saw many of their younger siblings. It shocked me to see how these "pesky" little brothers and sisters had come into their own. They had grown into strong and muscular teenagers, while for me the clock had stopped three summers ago. Back amongst a group of sixteen year-olds, sprawling over tattered overstuffed furniture, forever raiding the kitchen, mercilessly teasing each other to keep their hormones in check, it was all so familiar, yet so removed. When Chris Brun, the ranger who helped set up the program and who worked with us every day last year, arrived, the clamor of "Ranger Chris is here, Ranger Chris is here," made everything all right. It was like being back in summer camp.

We spent the first two days laying trees down along the stream bank to keep the cattle from crossing and destroying the riparian zone. All day long, the sound of the chain saw buzzed as the rangers thinned the forest while we hauled spindly pine trees down the steep hillside placing them along a one-and-a-half mile stretch of meandering stream. When we were finished, we attached netting along the bare areas to prevent further erosion and to allow the natural vegetation to return. We planted 1,500 seedlings and surveyed the work we had done the year before, documenting the changes that were taking place. At the end of each day, there was a satisfying feeling of having exhausted the body and of having accomplished something good. We swam in the lake where we were camped and stuffed ourselves with Wendy's fabulous fritatas. In the evening, we continued the tradition of hiking into the canyon to look for the Indian petroglyphs. Climbing high up on the rock face, gazing down the valley from this ancient site, watching the sun fade behind the distant hill—nature's reward.

I only stayed for a few days. I was able to transcend the pain I used to feel, knowing what I have done for Elana's memory and working with so many wonderful young people to help the environment. Being on the land, doing what she loved, was a way for her to live on. I could feel it in my heart. Last year there was just the darkness of her absence.

I don't think it is possible to truly heal without some memorial action. Otherwise the enormity of the loss remains locked inside and the child's death seems all too meaningless. Healing involves creating some good out of loss. I didn't know what this project would be like when I began, I don't know how it will evolve over time. But I do know, whatever the gift, whatever the giving, it comes out of the love I feel for her. It keeps the love alive.

Acceptance

Driving home late from work one evening shortly after the third anniversary of her death as a crisp fall wind scattered leaves on the ground, the Beatles' song "Let It Be" was playing on the radio. I've heard this song a hundred times over the last twenty years, but this day the words suddenly penetrated the ordinary. Breaking through the dullness of a familiar drive, it was like the voice of the angels singing, *"LET IT BE... LET IT BE... LET IT BE... LET IT BE...."* Plaintive, reconciling, surrendering. *"LET*

171

IT BE... LET IT BE... LET IT BE... LET IT BE". I gripped the steering wheel, turned up the volume all the way and sang along with everything in me. The road disappeared, fat salty tears streamed down my cheeks. I gave myself to this song.

An unexpected lesson in surrender, and it came driving down a dark freeway, on the radio. I knew that I had not really resolved what it meant to "accept" Elana's death. True, I was no longer enemies with what had occurred. True, I had accepted the reality of her physical absence, that she would not be coming home from college, would not be calling, that I had lost the future I would have had with her—there would be no wedding, no grandchildren, no mother-daughter odysseys. I had accepted these realities, for they were facts. But on some level, somewhere in my heart, I hadn't made my peace with what happened and I hadn't let her go. Somewhere inside, I still protested her death.

As I sang the refrain for the last time, its message imprinted on my brain, I finally understood, from the inside, that all I could do with Elana's death is to let it be. There is no place to put it, there is no ultimate meaning, it just is.

Now I no longer think about "accepting" Elana's death as some final turning point in my grieving. I no longer expect that ah! hah! moment when I will be reconciled. Losing a child is something you learn to live with. You don't really accept it, you don't get over it. Your relationship to it changes. As Stephen Levine, a Buddhist teacher, has written, letting go is a choiceless letting be.

There Are No Answers

We understand things little by little, we let go little by little. Healing doesn't reveal itself in grand gestures. I didn't resolve Elana's haunting last words until three years after her death. It didn't occur through a dramatic vision in the wilderness or some final insight from a high priest or shaman. It happened when I was sitting out on the deck quietly editing parts of this manuscript.

I was reading the section about my trip to Brazil. It was early morning when my head was clear. I came to the passage... "I left Brazil for the first time realizing that I may never know whether Elana's death was a random accident or part of her soul's journey." I re-read the passage thinking about the shamans, healers, and psychics I met in my travels and the contradictory information about whether Elana was an "innocent"in a plane crash or whether it was "her time." Suddenly, it hit me. For all my travels, for all my queries into other cultures and spiritual traditions, it was not that I *may* never know whether Elana's death was a random accident or part of her soul's journey, I WILL NEVER KNOW. With an overwhelming, immeasurable certainty, I finally got it. There is no definitive answer about what her last words meant. I can never know whether her death was a random accident or part of her soul's journey. I will never know whether I failed to heed a cosmic warning. I will never know if I could have saved her.

I finally understood what the rabbi meant the day of the funeral when he said there are no answers to the question WHY this happened, or why it happened to me. It is a question that goes nowhere. I guess I had to determine this for myself. To continue an endless inquiry into other cultures and religions in the hopes of finding an ultimate truth about the meaning of my daughter's death would be foolish. There are only sets of beliefs. Questions about death are non-reducible, they essentially remain unknowable. There is no answer to why bad things happen. There is only the meaning we will make out of our suffering.

In Rabbi Harold Kushner's book, *When Bad things happen to Good People,* he quotes the German theologian Dorothee Soelle, "the question is not where does the tragedy come from, but where does it lead." What good can come from such horror, what are its lessons, how can the world be made a better place?

I Should

There comes a time, when we say to ourselves we should rejoin the stream of life. I should go to that meeting, I should be on that committee. Enough time has gone by, one should make oneself get re-involved. But I had trouble forcing myself, the dates came and went, and I did nothing. Finally, when the first draft on this manuscript was in its final stages, I earnestly insisted, I really do need to be thinking about what will come after this. I decided to participate in curriculum planning for a new degree program in dispute resolution at Portland State University. I said it might be good for me. After all, I enjoyed teaching the five years I was on the faculty at the School of Social Work. As I was leaving for the meeting, I stepped off the curb landing with all my weight on the side of my ankle. Unable to move, I sat in the middle of the driveway for a long time until the throbbing subsided and I could hobble back into the house. That was the end of that.

The irony was interesting, but I was more amused than instructed. Later I thought, perhaps the wisdom of the body ultimately does lead us away from that which is not the right path. In my heart, I don't think I really wanted to go back to these previous endeavors.

Wounded Healer

It was the end of October and I had just returned from the third meeting of the shamanic training at the ranch in Sonoma. Inspired, I now knew I was moving in a different direction professionally, but didn't know exactly where or how.

The emotional energy behind the work I used to feel impassioned about was gone. I had been involved in the pioneering efforts in the field of mediation and alternative dispute resolution for almost fifteen years and had served as president of the national association. I had been on task forces, national committees and boards, had taught and done public speaking, and had recently published a book for separating couples on non-adversarial divorce. While I still valued the importance of alternative dispute resolution, it no longer had a sense of urgency for me. It was no longer a mission. I didn't care about the issues of the developing ADR profession or about advancing my career. What I cared about was being able to work with the depths, with a sense of the sacred, with healing. Through helping others from the very bowels of my own wound, from the compassion it had given me, I was healing myself. I didn't understand why this was so, just that it was.

I questioned my motivation. I asked myself why am I being drawn to Shamanism, to work with healing? What is it that I seek? As therapists, we are taught to be aware of our own motivation, of reasons for entering the helping professions so that our own need to rescue others, to feel important, or to be rescued, is not played out in our relationships with our patients. Healing work is different. You stand in your nakedness, in your woundedness, in the honesty of your own experience. You understand what it is to be broken by life and compassion comes not tinged with pity or fear, but with the knowledge of our common humanity. As you stand with another in that truth, there is an unspoken knowingness that transforms you both. I have heard it said that in a true healing relationship, both heal and are healed.

The wounded healer principle is an ancient one. We

can offer the most when it comes out of the understanding and compassion born of our own suffering. Out of this
place our real gifts can emerge.

As time went on, whether I sat with a tearful client
in therapy, mediated between angry and contentious
couples in the midst of divorce, or called upon my drum
and the healing powers of shamanism, I brought a dimension of heart to my clients that I hadn't known before.

Re-committing to Life

Richard and I were on a chartered bus to Mt. Hood
for a fiftieth birthday party when I ran into an old friend
and colleague whose daughter had been killed on a bi-
cycle ten years ago when she was nine. We had gotten
together a couple of times since Elana's death, but I was
so raw then; now I had a little more perspective. I remembered the first time we worked together shortly after his
daughter died. We were co-mediating the property settle-
ment in a divorce. The couple was arguing over capital
gains tax. Looking at him, I thought to myself, how can
you still be here, Ryan? Didn't you die too, how could you
work, how could you laugh, how can you think about someone else's capital gains tax. He told me that you have to
go on, you don't just stop. It was unimaginable to me at
the time that one survives the death of a child. Now I
know differently.

As the bus pulled out of the parking lot, we moved to
the back away from the laughter and champagne and
talked about what it has been like losing our daughters.
His way was to throw himself into work and let time heal.
I wanted to know how it had changed him because that
was what I was trying to figure out for myself. He described the same paradox I felt, a deeper appreciation of
life, but ultimately things didn't matter as they used to.
It was a sense of surrendering to a destiny, a Buddhist-
like non-attachment.

"It is easier to let things go," he said, "you are simply less attached. You see life in a different perspective after losing a child. You can't make the same assumptions, you don't take anything for granted. You don't try to control as much. You realize how little control we really have."

"Yeah," I said, "I know in the center of my being that there are no more endless tomorrows. Each day I'm aware that we are only here for the briefest of time. It has reordered my priorities, washed out the white noise. But I'm not a Buddhist, and this feeling of not being attached to life in the way I was before leaves me unsettled."

Ryan reminded me to give myself more time. We all come back in our own way.

Was I back? Something was emerging from the ashes, but it had an uneasy unsteady form. I didn't recognize it as myself. I kept looking in the mirror and wondering. I remember having read last year in a book about grief that there is a point where the mourner must recommit to life. At the time, not only had I not re-committed to life, I didn't want to. I was still a spectator. I hadn't yet decided that I had a right to be here when my daughter was not. As I talked with Ryan, I realized that I still had not made a conscious decision to fully embrace life. But it is not about whether I feel I have the right to be here. It is more a sense of our impermanence. There is an awareness of life's transience that had soaked through. It has become the eyes through which I see the world now.

Perhaps there is a point of wholly embracing life again. I really don't know. Maybe the real wisdom lies in what Joseph Campbell meant when he said we must commit to life even though we recognize it will devour us.

The Power of Love

I had often heard that the basis of all spiritual and healing work is love. I had read stories about bereaved parents who spoke of still having the child's love in their heart. I didn't get it. I thought, how could you could open your heart and have it filled with love when your life had vaporized before your very eyes? How could you possibly keep love in a heart that has been shattered? It was a paradox I couldn't comprehend. I suppose I had to live through it to understand. You have to be utterly and completely broken by life, to have raged against the fates, allowed sorrow, anger and bitterness their reign, have tried everything else, to realize that the only thing that heals is love. It is something you learn only by coming out the other side.

To some extent, without realizing it, I didn't know what else to do but have an open heart. When I felt angry and unforgiving, it caused me more pain. When we were dealing with the insurance companies, lawyers, the FAA reports and the other families, I started to develop an ulcer. The anger I felt would begin to rip apart my insides. It wasn't worth it. My pain was enormous enough. There was no room for more.

For the longest time, everything I had read about the relationship of love and healing was just an abstraction. I can't say how it came to be in my bones. Perhaps it was my trip to Brazil. Being near the Amazon, "the lungs of the earth," meeting uncommon individuals, people of the highest integrity who generously shared their gifts of healing, experiencing how love can be channeled as an energetic force that can penetrate and heal. Or perhaps, it was the mini-sabbatical in Bali where I experienced a way of life in harmony with natural world. These experiences took hold of something deep in my psyche, and this heart that had been cracked open by grief has remained open to love in a way it never had before.

One comes to see that there is no choice but to love. When I succumbed to self-pity in the face of other's joys, if I became bitter when I saw friend's children move into experiences and adventures that Elana would never have, I'd withdraw and close myself off. This ultimately led to greater anguish.

An open heart lets loving energy in. A closed heart eventually seals and the life force dies.

Bad Days

I can still have bad days. Now they can take me by surprise. As time goes on you forget how much missing your child can hurt. For me, it begins in anticipation of her birthday, my birthday, Mother's Day, the holidays, the anniversary of her death. I become sad and lifeless and don't care much about anything. I don't have my daughter returning for Thanksgiving from college, I have my tears. It is as if they never left.

Cranky and angry, I want to be left alone. I want to blame someone, but there is no one to blame. I find myself thinking it's not fair, even though I know better. I walk around with a scowl on my face. I say to myself, it has been three years since she died, I should not be feeling this way. But I do.

As the third Thanksgiving approached, the feeling of dread invaded my psyche as the November page turned on my calendar. When the day arrived, it wasn't so bad. We were making Thanksgiving dinner and friends were coming over. Richard's son, who is the age Elana would be, was home from college and his daughter, now a high school junior, Elana's age when she died, was watching TV. I went out for a run as I had every Thanksgiving before dinner. Cool, misty, wet, a typical Oregon November day. I don't know where it came from, but I started to sob almost as soon as I hit the pavement. I thought about all the other times I had run this wooded two-lane road in front of my house—with friends, with Elana, by myself. I had run through my divorce, through each of my parent's deaths, through the rain, the snow, and on glorious spring mornings when life held nothing but promise. I don't run anymore because of my knees, except on Thanksgiving. I

179

needed to be by myself where I could cry into the wind, let the rain wash over my tears, where I could call out loud, "Elana, where are you?" and no one would hear me.

When I came back from the run, I sat in the rose garden not caring that I was getting wet, crying about Elana until I didn't need to anymore. Muddy, soaked to the bone, but spiritually cleansed, I went into the house and got ready for dinner.

Bad days come and go. They don't sink me the way they used to, they don't linger as long. I think they will always be there. They are the legacy of love.

Saying Goodbye

I have not said goodbye to Elana, but I think it is something I someday must do. We must say goodbye to our child, goodby to the future he or she won't have, to the future we won't have. Even if we anticipated the death and held our child close at the end, I think it takes a long time to release them to their fate, to see their fate as different from ours, something we no longer have control over. Again, the rabbi's words at the funeral echo in my mind: *Children are but gifts, they are lent to us, they do not come with guarantees.* Those were just words to me then. Now I know them to be true.

I still have not dismantled Elana's room. It has been over three years. I can conceive of doing it because we could use the space, but I still can't make myself do it. I am afraid that in dismantling her room, I would erase her presence.

I don't know how I will say goodbye to Elana, but something inside tells me it is the final act of my healing. Like the time twenty years ago in a Gestalt therapy seminar when I sat facing an empty chair, sobbing and saying goodbye to my husband and my marriage. Had it not been for that experience, I would not know how utterly painful, but also liberating, saying goodbye can be.

But everything in me resists. Perhaps it will come as it did with the goodbye to my marriage—an empty chair, her picture, a tearful conversation, a hug, then direct, unequivocally, like jumping off the high diving board, "Elana I love you and I release you."

EPILOGUE: The Other Side of the Mountain

A day of reconciliation came. It happened as the first glow of morning light rose over a silhouetted mountain in the Mohave desert almost four years after Elana's death. It was unexpected. I was at a reunion of the people from my three-year Shamanic training program. We were at a ranch in the desert, an oasis of flower and fauna, set amidst the brown grays of thistle and cactus stretching out across the parched, thirsty landscape. Taking refuge from the afternoon heat in the dark cool interior of the lodge, we closed our eyes asking for guidance in preparation for an all-night ceremony. A forgotten dream of the night before suddenly came back to me. In the dream, Elana appeared as the twenty year-old she would have been and said she was going to move into an apartment this summer with Chessy and Kate. I told her that she hadn't asked permission and that I was unprepared for her to have a life so separate from my own. She told me this was what she was going to do. The rent was free and I could come see the apartment which was above some little shops, where in fact her friends had rented an apartment for the summer. I told her I wasn't ready for this. She assured me it would be all right, she wasn't leaving, we would still visit. Then, just as she was about to take me to see the apartment, I woke up.

As I recalled this dream deep in meditation, the voices of spirit came. *It was time*, they said. *I had to release her.* Nothing in my ordinary consciousness would have compelled me to do this, because everything in my ordinary consciousness resisted. But this was the voice of a higher reality, a higher knowing and the insistence and piercing truth of this guidance was absolutely compelling. I was being told I had to let her go, but that it would be all right, I had to trust I wouldn't lose her. As I lay there with my eyes closed, I saw myself hugging her goodbye, kissing her, saying the words, "I release you, dear sweet Elana." Tears streamed down my face as if this was real. I knew a final reconciliation was to come in this long night under the desert sky.

Just before sunset, we walked up the mountain to a plateau at the foot of the canyon. We honored the sun, singing its praises and drumming in gratitude. The fire keepers ritually lit the sacred fire and we sat around it as darkness fell. A large mother drum sounded all night as four people at a time beat the songs and prayers inspired by being on this land. Lying back and journeying to the stars, feeling the gentle wind dance in all directions, sharing food, listening to the distant coyotes call, the ancient rhythms of the drum in the background, thinking about the ceremonies we performed to honor the land, I wondered is this what gatherings of the clans were like long ago? Is this the sense of community and communion modern souls hunger for?

About four a.m. when the new moon began to rise on the eastern horizon, I took my drum and walked down the hill away from the group. I stood in silence as the warm desert night and serenading breeze wove a spell. High on this sandy plateau, a vista of cactus, juniper and sagebrush, ethereal and full of mystery unfolding all around me, the constellations in startling contrast to a velvet sky above me, and the first light of daybreak peering over the distant mountains. I gazed at it all entranced. We are so small, it is so big, and she is out here somewhere. I started singing quietly and beating my drum. The words and chant just came...*Elana can you hear me calling your name, Elana can you hear me calling, Elana can you hear me calling you name, Elana can you hear me calling. Elana, lana, lana, lana. Elana, lana, lana, lana.* Rhythmically moving in place to the beat of the drum, I sang this song over and over as I stared deeply into the mysteries of this desert night, the dark silhouette of the mountains holding me like a magnet. Soon I was beating the drum with everything that was in me, then, falling to my knees softly, quietly, almost a whisper...*Elana can you hear me calling your name, Elana can you hear me calling...Elana can you hear me calling your name, Elana can you hear me calling....* Every emotion moved through that drum. I don't know how long I stood there. It could have been an hour, it could have been a day.

Watching the horizon turn crimson against the silhouette of the distant mountain peaks as they rose from the valley floor, peering into a window of eternity as the cycle of another new dawn welcomed us, I could finally see. I finally came to accept that she was there, in a place different from me. She was in a place I couldn't go. She was on the other side of the mountain. It was undeniable, unalterable and incontestable. Tears streaming, I cried to her and into the night as I sank to my knees, fingers digging into the earth, proclaiming to the dawn with all my being, that I will accept this. *I ACCEPT THAT SHE IS ON THE OTHER SIDE OF THE MOUNTAIN, AND I AM HERE.* Exhausted, relieved, a sinking feeling in my heart, I held my head in my hands. When I looked up, the star of Venus bright as a rocket was rising under the crescent moon just as it had the morning of her funeral. Was this the gift the spirits had foretold, the sign that says even in death I am not leaving you? Standing there surrendering to the beauty of the morning star against the backlit sky, a deep calm came over me.

I walked back to the campfire and picked up the red rose that had been lying on the altar in remembrance of Elana. I caressed the delicate petals and inhaled the sweet fragrance. Soon I was gazing at its flawless form with my other eyes. Its essence was her essence. She became the rose. I held it to my breast, and she entered my heart in the enigmatic beauty of a simple rose. From that moment she was transformed from just a loss into a presence.

Now it is as if she resides somewhere else deep in my soul, in the breeze that gently caresses my face as I lay back looking up at the tree tops swaying against a cloudless blue sky, in the birds that seem to change their song and turn their heads toward me when I call out her name, in the night sky, black and full of mystery. I know she is out there somewhere.

Everything I touch in my life that has any importance or meaning is touched by her. From firming the soil around the flowers that find their new home in my garden each year, to my awe at the enormous old willow trees in front of farm houses on back country roads, to the compassion I feel for others who have suffered tragedy, to the deep desire to somehow want to be of service.

Her death has given me deeper eyes, lifted the veil of our separateness, allowed me entry into the immensity of divine love, given me glimpses of eternity. My tears have joined the river of tears. I am who I am now because of her, and the loving presence I bring to everything is her final gift to me.

> *"All things must pass; all that lives must die. All that we prize is but lent to us and the time comes when we must surrender it. We are travelers on the same road that leads to the same end."*

— from the Mourner's Kaddish